"Tanya's come-hither cookbook inspired both the armchair traveler and the armchair chowhound in me. Reading it, I imagined the pleasure of living in West Oakland, having a regular seat of my own at Brown Sugar's counter, and ordering up my favorite dishes without even having to look at the menu. With this book in hand, I know that every choice is a winner."

—Sara Moulton, host of *Sara's Weeknight Meals* on public television

"Brown Sugar Kitchen is the gathering point and center of the West Oakland community not only because of the generous hospitality but the great food that nurtures and binds folks. The *Brown Sugar Kitchen* cookbook not only reflects this warm community, but Tanya shares her recipes for dishes you will want to make again and again. For me just learning how to make Bacon-Cheddar–Green Onion Biscuits and Cornmeal Waffles with Apple Cider Syrup will make the *Brown Sugar Kitchen* cookbook a frequent guest at my table."

—Bruce Aidells, author of *The Great Meat Cookbook*

TANYA HOLLAND

WITH JAN NEWBERRY

BROWN SUGAR KITCHEN

NEW-STYLE, DOWN-HOME RECIPES
FROM SWEET WEST OAKLAND

WITH EDITORIAL HELP FROM PHIL SURKIS

FOREWORD BY
MICHAEL CHABON

PHOTOGRAPHS BY JODY HORTON

CHRONICLE BOOKS
SAN FRANCISCO

Library of Congress Cataloging-in-Publication Data available.

ISBN 978-1-4521-2234-2

Manufactured in China

Designed by Alice Chau
Typesetting by Howie Severson

Prop styling by Kate LeSueur. Many thanks to Heath Ceramics for the dishes
on pages 76, 78, 154, and 178.
Food styling by Kate LeSueur and Tanya Holland

Angostura aromatic bitters is a registered trademark of Angostura Limited.
Burlesque bitters is a registered trademark of Bitterman's Inc.
Buffalo Trace bourbon is a registered trademark of Buffalo Trace Distillery.
Dry Soda is a registered trademark of Dry SODA Co.
Four Roses Bourbon is a registered trademark of Four Roses Distillery LLC.
Gosling's Black Seal Bermuda Rum is a registered trademark of Gosling Brothers, Ltd.
Gran Classico Bitter is a registered trademark of Tempus Fugit Spirits.
Heinz Chili Sauce is a registered trademark of H.J. Heinz Co.
Tabasco is a registered trademark of McIlhenny Company.

10 9 8 7 6 5 4 3

Chronicle Books LLC
680 Second Street
San Francisco, California 94107
www.chroniclebooks.com

To my parents,
Hollis and Annette Holland

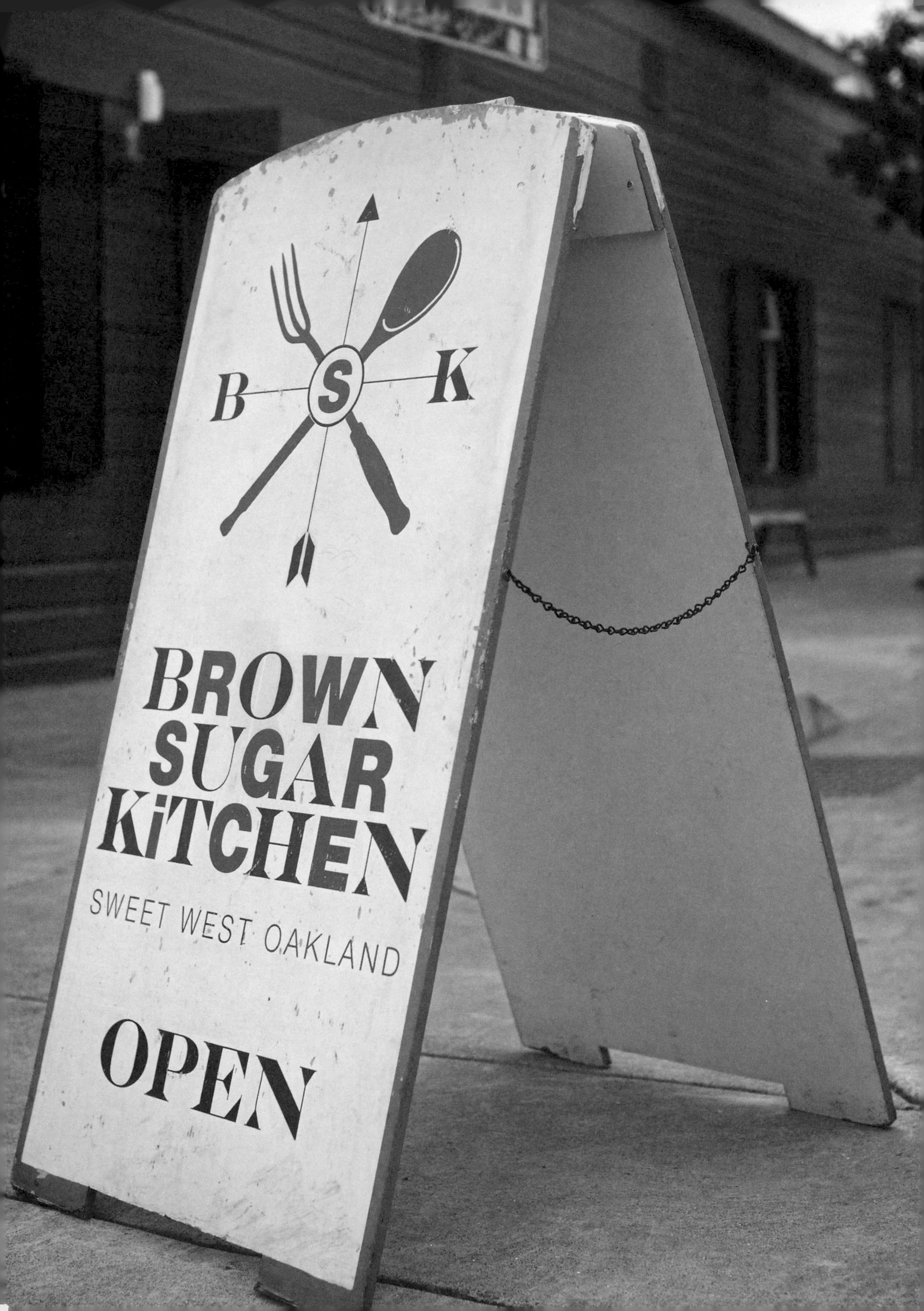
B S K
BROWN
SUGAR
KiTCHEN
SWEET WEST OAKLAND
OPEN

CONTENTS

FOREWORD

BY MICHAEL CHABON

Oakland—like a swinging party, like an emergency—is happening. Oakland is *always* happening. From the moment of its founding, in the 1850s, by a nefarious confederation of squatters, opportunists, filibusterers, graft artists, boosters, visionary thieves and confidence men, Bump City has been happening. And yet, in all that time, Oakland has never quite *happened.* Or rather, Oakland never *has happened.* Oakland has never had its day. It has never gone soft, grown fat, rested on its laurels. It has never entirely gotten its act together, remembered to set its alarm clock, made it through to payday, waited for its cake to cool completely. There *is* a there there (Oakland coolly says "Bite me" to Gertrude Stein); but Oakland's not there yet.

Getting there, though. Oakland is—always, forever—getting there.

Oakland is like America, in that way. Oakland's like America in a lot of ways—violent and peace-loving, burdened by a calamitous racial history, factious and muddled, friendly and casual, rich in local genius and in natural beauty, poorly governed, sweet-natured, cold-eyed, out to lunch, out for blood, out for a good time. And, above all, *promising.* Every day, Oakland makes and breaks the American promise, a promise so central to the idea of America that we carry it around everywhere we go, in our wallets, jingling in our pockets. I mean, of course, *E pluribus unum*: Out of all

the scattered sparks, one shining light. It's a utopian promise, and like all utopian promises, liable to breakage. But even if that promise can never truly be redeemed, it can be—it must be—endlessly *renewed.* And it's the work that we put in, day after day, toward renewing the promise, not the promise's fulfillment, that really matters.

Tanya Holland knows that. Every day, starting at 5:30 A.M., she renews Oakland's promise at Brown Sugar Kitchen, a little hip-pocket utopia in the city's wild west end. Of all the many good restaurants, greasy-spoon to top-drawer, that make up a substantial share of the cultural wealth of Oakland, Tanya's Brown Sugar Kitchen most clearly, most faithfully, and most thrillingly embodies, one plate of chicken and waffles at a time, the ongoing, ever-renewed promise of the city she has come to love and, in a very real sense, to embody.

Drop by Brown Sugar Kitchen any day, for breakfast or lunch, and you will find people of all ages and stations, professing various brands of faith or doubt, tracing their ancestries to Africa and Europe, Asia and South America, to the Cherokee, Shawnee or Creek. You might very well find all those inheritances gathered around a single table, perhaps even in the genetic code of a single member of the waitstaff.

Diversity in the kitchen and dining room is hardly unusual in an Oakland restaurant, of course—that's one of the things to love about Oakland. Even in cities segregated far more determinedly than Oakland, I've noticed that a popular soul-food restaurant will often feature the most integrated tables in town—that's one of the things to love about soul food. Beans, rice and collards are a powerful force for transformation. But the crowd's different at Brown Sugar Kitchen. More jumbled, the lines of race and class drawn more faintly than in Oakland's other restaurants, soul-food or otherwise. A more purposive clientele, I want to say, *self*-jumbled, everybody showing up with his or her own eraser to rub away at those lines a little more. One of the most beautiful things about human beings, in the midst of so much that is ugly, is the desire that takes hold of us, if only we can manage to leave our homes, our villages and our little worlds behind, for the companionship of people from Elsewhere. Make no mistake; people come to Brown Sugar Kitchen for the food. I believe that I could be hauled back from the gates of the Underworld by the prospect of a bowl of Tanya's shrimp and grits. But it was Oakland and not some other town, remember, that cradled the visions of the most high prophet Sly Stone, and to a greater extent than I've found in other American cities, the Everyday People of Oakland are hip to the possibility that the point of the journey is neither the destination *nor* the journey itself but rather the coming to a crossroads, to a watering hole, to what my character Archy

Stallings, in *Telegraph Avenue,* likes to call a "caravansary." The point of the journey, to the everyday wanderer, is the feeling one gets on crossing the threshold of one of those magical places along the way, built on the borderline between here and there, where the stories and the homelands and the crooked routes of history come together in a slice of sweet potato pie.

Maybe the word I'm looking for to describe the spirit that imbues the patrons and the principals of Brown Sugar Kitchen is something more like "mindfulness." (An East Bay word if there ever was one.) As lovers of Oakland, Tanya and her husband, Phil Surkis, are *mindful* that the neighborhood where they chose to build their caravansary is the broken heart of Oakland, the place where all those industrious scoundrels who afterward lent their names to streets and civic buildings first conspired to defraud the Peralta family of their land. All the paths of ancestry and migration taken by Oakland's founding peoples—Indian, Spanish, Mexican, Anglo-, Asian-, and African-American—are densely knotted in West Oakland, with its physical routes and roadways, its boulevards and streets. West Oakland is the great crossroads of the city's history, the stage and the scene of its starkest crimes and dramas, its most tragic comedies, from the founding land-grab to the glory of the Pullman strikes, from the apocalyptic destruction rained down by federal urban policy in the '60s to the collapse

of the Great Beast of Urban Renewal, the Cypress Freeway, during the Loma Prieta earthquake of 1989. The Black Panthers, the Oakland Oaks, shipbuilders and railway workers, immigrant Jews and Portuguese, Okies and followers of the Great Migration, all came and went along Market and Cypress and West Street, as neighborhoods rose and fell, and Huey P. Newton got murdered, and the industrial demands of two world wars brought a measure of security and comfort, often for the first time, to people whose status had been marginal and precarious. Tanya and Phil were mindful, in choosing the site for their caravansary, that there could be no better place than along the Mandela Parkway, the enchanted road that grew up, gracious and wide and landscaped with greenery, in the gap that had once been the dark underbelly of the Cypress Freeway.

Tanya showed the same mindfulness in conceiving her Kitchen, in formulating her recipes, in committing herself to the cooking of soul food. This was, by her own admission, an unexpected choice. She had come west with plans to open a place that would showcase her La Varenne training; but then she dialed in to the local vibe, to the Sly Stone vision, to that Oakland state of mind. And one day she found herself standing on the 2500 block of the Mandela Parkway, feeling those paths of ancestry, those trails and roads and streets and railheads all coming together in the great

soul terminus of West Oakland, and determined to set up shop, there, along the banks of the Mandela, and lay down her own artful and inspired version of the Oakland promise in the form of po' boys, roux, and waffles.

Consciously or intuitively—mindfully—Tanya made this culinary choice, I believe, because the cuisine we know as soul food—so styled sometime in the 1950s, around the time rhythm and blues was becoming *soul music*—comes closer than any other product of American art and ingenuity to redeeming the promise of *E pluribus unum*. Peanuts, rice, okra and yams from Africa; Central American beans and cassava; European pork, cabbage, molasses and turnips; Indian corn and hominy, berries and greens: soul food is the caravansary along the road from the African past to the American present, from freedom to slavery to freedom again. Soul food is the little joint at the broken heart of America where all the kitchen inheritances ingather, and get tangled like travelers' yarns, like the paths of exile and homecoming, like strands of DNA. From the day she opened her little utopia on the Mandela Parkway, Tanya has been making and keeping and redeeming her promise: Come on in, all of you everyday wanderers, and take a seat, and I will feed your soul. Oh—and come hungry.

WELCOME TO BROWN SUGAR KITCHEN

I am not a morning person, and yet I've seen sunrise almost every day for the past six years. I'm thankful I live only four blocks from Brown Sugar Kitchen because I can be in the kitchen before I realize how tired I am.

I'm the first to arrive, circling the pie-shaped building at 5:30 A.M., removing the heavy-duty locks from the window grates and doors. As soon as I walk in, I turn on the ovens and fire up the burners. I'm awake now—sleepiness and fire don't mix. Pulling out a rondeau pot, I fill it with oil for frying chicken. Then I fill another shallow pot with water and a big splash of distilled white vinegar—ground zero for poaching eggs. Assembling the pots and pans is one of the rituals that help me set the tone for the day.

I throw a few oversize tea bags into a pot of hot water to steep for chai, and get another pot of water boiling so I can cook the grits (with great care and love, of course, the two most important ingredients). Into the ovens go the sticky buns that were prepared the day before, and left to come to room temperature on a shelf above the stove. This opening routine takes ninety minutes. It's like yoga or meditation, but with coffee and sticky buns. No, I'm not a morning person, but I've come to love the early shift. I call it, "Getting the party started right."

Just before six, the building shakes as the first deliveries arrive. We know when the trucks pull up because our single-story wood-framed building starts to vibrate. A driver wheels in a hand truck stacked with boxes of produce. I know all the delivery drivers, because I see each of them several times a week. We have no walk-in, just a couple of stand-alone refrigerators. With so little storage space, we cycle through our entire stock of ingredients every few days. This constant receiving of goods makes me feel like an annex of the Port of Oakland, our neighbor at the other end of the street. Most restaurants can stock their pantries and coolers with enough ingredients to get them through the week, but Brown Sugar Kitchen is not like most restaurants.

Our first server enters the scene right at six, unstacking the chairs from the tabletops, lining up the napkins and silverware with great precision, setting out the Tabasco and Crystal hot sauces, and pulling the jars of our house-made jam from the fridge. As much as I'd love a cup of coffee by now, we don't start brewing until just before we open, grinding the beans to order for each pot.

I keep an eye on the clock as it inches toward seven, making sure I stay on track. I'm a stickler for consistency, and it's important that the restaurant is ready to go when the doors open. I may be stirring the last of the Cheddar into the pot of grits, but if an order is placed at 7:01, it will be on the table by 7:06.

Around 6:30, I fire up one of the playlists that my husband, Phil, has made. Nina Simone starts to sing and my movements become more fluid. I love to dance. Guests might see me on the line and think I'm cooking, but I'm really feeling the music, feeling the timing—dancing and cooking at the same time.

Now it's time to turn on the waffle irons. They need a good thirty minutes to heat up; they'll be running nonstop for the next eight hours. I pull a tub of waffle batter out of the refrigerator, where it's been rising overnight. One tub holds enough batter for about fifteen waffles and we sometimes have up to twenty tubs ready to go because I simply cannot stand to run out of anything.

Next I turn my attention to the fried chicken. It's been soaking in a buttermilk-herb bath since yesterday afternoon. I take the chicken pieces out of the buttermilk, toss them in a bin of seasoned flour, and *carefully* transfer them to the pot of bubbling oil. (It looks scary, but I'm used to it.) If the oil splashes up and burns my thumb, I'm reminded of what I tell my cooks: "There comes a point when you stop cutting yourself, but you never stop getting burned."

While the chicken fries, my multitasking frenzy reaches a crescendo: I fill a pie shell with sweet-potato filling; add grits to the boiling water; dump a bin of potatoes on the

flat-top grill. I grab a pastry brush and paint the tops of the biscuits with cream before putting them in the oven. There's a rhythm to the work, and I rely on my internal clock more than timers. I know exactly when the sticky buns are done, when the chicken needs to be pulled, and when the biscuits are tender but not yet browned.

At ten minutes to seven a few cars are already lined up at the curb. Then customers' faces start to populate the windows, with their noses pressed to the glass. It's time. Right at seven, I slip on my chef's coat, just as our server carries the bulky "Open" sandwich board to the curb. As customers stream in, I transfer a tray of fried chicken to the oven to keep it warm and ready for that first chicken and waffles order, which I know will be coming at 7:03.

———————————

Brown Sugar Kitchen isn't the restaurant I intended to open. I had plans for a bistro where I would serve steak frites, bouillabaisse, braised short ribs—the food I fell in love with when I studied cooking in France. I imagined that restaurant on a busy corner in downtown Oakland, Boston, Manhattan, Brooklyn—one of the many cities where I've lived—with high ceilings and big windows that would flood the dining room with natural light. The tables would be set with nice glassware, heavy flatware, and big bistro plates. The wine list would be thick and bound in leather. Somewhere in one of the corners there would be a booth for VIPs or a line of banquettes for comfortable and sometimes private seating. Diners would eat in courses: an appetizer and main course followed by dessert. Perhaps there would even be an amuse-bouche sent from the kitchen.

A soul-food restaurant on an isolated corner in West Oakland was not part of the plan. But then Phil and I moved to the neighborhood. Phil insists that he bought our home based on the "vibe." (Acting on gut is a quality we share.) It wasn't until after we had moved in that we discovered there wasn't even a place to get a cup of coffee within walking distance. The one restaurant in the neighborhood was a Jamaican diner called the Island Café. People here still talk about the jerk chicken, but it was clear to us that the owner was struggling. Though an "Open" sign was permanently bolted to the side of the building, the café was almost always closed. We had a sense that the owner might want out, so we approached him about taking over the lease, and were able to make a deal.

The lot that the restaurant sits on is exposed on all sides—it's literally an island. Mandela Parkway had just been landscaped with trees, and this newly lush parkway was the only green in what was otherwise a barren land-scape. Our neighbors are a storage facility,

a forklift company, and an auto repair shop. There were no other retail businesses for a couple of miles. On paper, opening a restau-rant in West Oakland did not look like a good idea. But I knew our restaurant had potential. I lived in New York City in the 1980s, where I witnessed the possibilities of change first-hand. I felt the possibilities of West Oakland.

As an executive chef, I've inherited a lot of kitchens, and most of them were in need of a very thorough cleaning. But this was the cleanest restaurant kitchen I'd ever seen. I was beside myself with joy. Instead of scrubbing grease off the walls, I focused on the fun things, like paint colors. I picked my favorites—split-pea green and chocolate brown, to play off the orange linoleum floor and the black countertop. Then we installed a dozen gooseneck light fixtures on the sides of the building. Our neigh-bors were thrilled, as the additional lighting made the area safer.

I figured we'd start slow, with a short menu of coffee and baked goods and hours limited to just breakfast and lunch. With just fifty seats, I would've been pleased to serve 500 people a week.

As Phil likes to tell the story, I had the entire menu in my head and put it on paper just days before we opened. The equipment and the lim-ited amount of space dictated what we could serve. But there was a wood-fired rotisserie smoker in the back, plus room for at least one waffle iron, a small fryer, a commercial griddle, and a six-burner cooktop on top of two conventional ovens. We had four refrigerators of varying sizes and a small freezer. I never planned on having frozen ingredients anyway, so I don't miss having a freezer. Back then, it seemed like we had so much room in those refrigerators—more than we would ever be able to fill. I hired one dishwasher, two cooks, and three servers.

We opened our doors on January 15, 2008, Martin Luther King Jr.'s birthday—an auspicious day for a start, I thought. Phil was still working as a claims adjuster then and took the day off to be with us. He joined in as I gathered the staff in a circle, said a prayer, and opened the door. Our first customer, Dave Worden, walked through the door and asked for a cup of coffee. The entire staff descended in an attempt to impress him with our fabulous service. I guess we did all right because he's become a regular customer. We did thirty-seven covers on that Tuesday. By Saturday, we had a waiting list for brunch and served 100 people. These days, we sometimes serve more than 400 customers on a Saturday.

On that bright January morning, it never occurred to me that I would be cooking lunch for the mayor and serving gumbo to Stewart Copeland of the Police. I wouldn't have believed it if you had told me that Taj Mahal and Ledisi would be regulars at my restaurant.

Brown Sugar Kitchen has become more than just a restaurant, it's a community. We're an anchor for the neighborhood, a canteen for the artists, truckers, and tradesmen who work here. We're a business that hires locally, a place where a young cook can learn and go on to become a chef. We buy our coffee, produce, and even our wine from Oakland producers, and we're a fund-raising venue that supports neighborhood organizations.

We've become a destination, too, drawing customers from far beyond the Oakland border. I like to think that when people come to Brown Sugar Kitchen for the first time they see beyond the stereotype of West Oakland as a dangerous, dirty place. That they see what I see when I come to work—a dynamic, diverse community brought together by a shared appetite for fried chicken and for the kind of connections that food can forge.

But of all the things about Brown Sugar Kitchen that I take pride in—the lightness of our waffles, the skill of my cooks, and the hospitality of our servers—the part of my job that brings me the most satisfaction is the people who eat here. Look around our dining room and you'll see African Americans, Asian Americans, and Latino Americans. Infants and the elderly, gay people and straight, celebrities and day laborers, bankers and emerging artists and musicians all sit at our tables—sometimes they share the same table. I have no idea what it is, but something happens when people come to Brown Sugar Kitchen, and the differences that divide suddenly become the things that draw them together. Defenses drop and curiosity takes over. Judgments fade and alliances are born. I feel lucky to be a part of it.

West Oakland is more than just a place where we live. It's our home now, and we can't imagine living anywhere else. People say that I've changed West Oakland, but the truth is, West Oakland has changed me.

TANYA HOLLAND

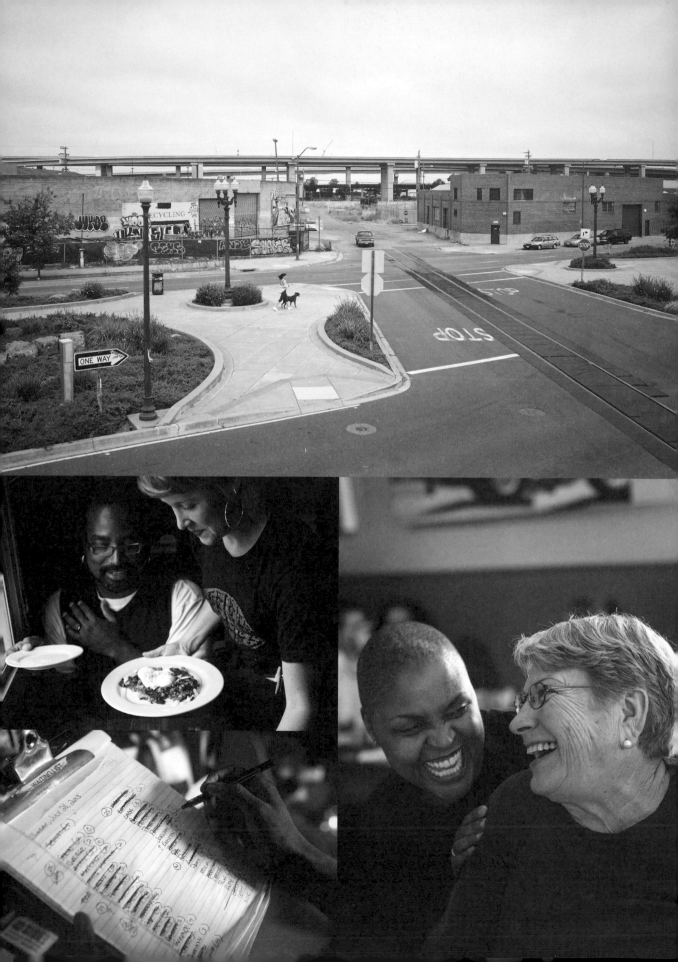

CHAPTER 1
BREAKFAST
& BRUNCH

I love that moment in the early morning when the first customers stumble through the door. People are a little more raw at that hour, slightly less polished than they'll be after they've had their coffee and a bite to eat. From my spot cooking behind the line, I can watch the steady trickle of guests filling the tables; there are always some new faces as well as old ones. People from the neighborhood stop in for a sticky bun or a scone on their way to work; others take a table for an early morning meeting or maybe just some time alone with the newspaper. Working the line in an open kitchen allows me to keep an eye on who's coming in, and if it's one of our regulars, a chance to catch up. Quite a few of our customers have standard orders that never vary. I can often get their breakfast started before the menus even hit the table.

Our morning menu is short, a tight list of favorites we know our customers crave. And I love how so many of our regulars always order the same thing. Mildred must have her granola, and Jeff will be upset if we don't have smoked pork hash (we've run out two or three times in the past few years). Before I opened the restaurant I imagined that I would change the menu more often, but I know better now. If I don't keep it exactly as it is, my customers wouldn't be able to start their days right.

Many of the recipes here are—in true Southern style—on the hearty side, such as our legendary waffles, a big bowl of shrimp and grits, or hash and eggs. All will easily fill you up until lunch and beyond. But there are lighter options, too, like our nutty granola and a vegetable tart with a side salad.

CORNMEAL WAFFLES WITH APPLE CIDER SYRUP

These waffles are based on the rise-overnight, yeasted version made famous by the late cooking teacher and cookbook author Marion Cunningham. I added cornmeal to the batter to give them a distinctive Southern flavor and make them my own. Now they're one of Brown Sugar Kitchen's signature dishes and it's impossible to imagine the restaurant without them. The apple cider syrup is an homage to my grandmother, who always fried apples for breakfast; it's a nice change from the ubiquitous maple syrup. These waffles have received a lot of press, with perhaps my favorite review coming from the Pulitzer Prize–winning food writer Jonathan Gold, who says they are worth the five-and-a-half-hour drive from Los Angeles. I'll let the recipe do the talking.

APPLE CIDER SYRUP

1½ CUPS/300 G firmly packed brown sugar

1½ TSP apple cider vinegar

4 CUPS/960 ML apple cider

2 cinnamon sticks

½ CUP/115 G unsalted butter

WAFFLES

2 TSP active dry yeast

¾ CUP/180 ML warm water

3 eggs

3 CUPS/720 ML whole milk

1 CUP/140 G cornmeal

2 CUPS/255 G all-purpose flour

1½ TSP kosher salt

1½ TSP granulated sugar

¾ CUP/170 G unsalted butter, melted

Vegetable oil for the waffle iron

½ TSP baking soda

To make the syrup: In a large pot, combine the brown sugar, vinegar, cider, cinnamon, and butter. Bring to a boil, reduce to a simmer, and let cook until reduced to 1½ cups/360 ml, about 45 minutes. Discard the cinnamon and keep warm over very low heat. (To make ahead, refrigerate in an airtight container for up to 1 month.)

To make the waffles: In a small bowl, combine the yeast and warm water. Let stand until foamy, about 10 minutes. In a large bowl, whisk together the eggs and milk. In another large bowl, sift together the cornmeal, flour, salt, and granulated sugar. Add the yeast mixture to the eggs and milk, then whisk in the flour mixture until thoroughly combined. Whisk in the melted butter until just combined. Cover the bowl with plastic wrap, and refrigerate for at least 4 hours or up to overnight.

Preheat the oven to 250°F/120°C. Preheat the waffle iron and brush lightly with oil. Set a wire rack over a baking sheet.

CONTINUED

Remove the waffle batter from the refrigerator and stir in the baking soda. Ladle some of the batter into the waffle iron, close the lid, and cook the waffles until golden and cooked through, about 3 minutes or according to the manufacturer's instructions. Transfer the waffle to the rack to keep warm in the oven. Repeat with the remaining batter, placing the waffles in a single layer on the rack.

Serve the waffles warm with warm apple cider syrup.

BACON-CHEDDAR-GREEN ONION BISCUITS

Buttermilk biscuits should be buttery and flaky. It's the way the dough is handled that contributes to these qualities more than anything else. The butter should be cold and the dough shouldn't be overworked. I realize that adding bacon, cheese, and green onions pushes these savory biscuits right over the top, but in this case that turns out to be a very good thing. We bake hundreds of these a week. Our regulars who rush in for a cup of coffee know they can also grab one of these biscuits if they need a small bite but can't wait for anything else.

Preheat the oven to 425°F/220°C. Line two baking sheets with parchment paper.

Using a stand mixer fitted with the paddle attachment, combine the flour, baking powder, salt, and baking soda and mix briefly on low speed just to combine. Add the chilled butter and continue mixing on low speed until the butter is cut into pea-size pieces. Drizzle in the buttermilk and mix just until the dough forms a ball. Divide the dough into thirds.

In a small bowl, combine the Cheddar, bacon, and green onions. On a lightly floured surface and with a lightly floured rolling pin, roll out one piece of dough to an 11-by-8½-in/28-by-21.5-cm rectangle and sprinkle with half of the Cheddar mixture. Roll out another piece of dough to an 11-by-8½-in/28-by-21.5-cm rectangle and layer on top of the dough with the Cheddar mixture. Sprinkle the second layer of dough with the remaining half of the Cheddar mixture. Roll out the remaining piece of dough and layer it on top. Gently roll out the dough layers to make a 12-by-10-in/30.5-by-25-cm rectangle.

Using a 2-in/5-cm biscuit cutter, stamp out 18 biscuits and set them on the prepared baking sheets. Brush the tops with cream. Bake until just starting to turn golden but before the bottoms begin to brown, about 15 minutes. Let cool slightly and serve warm.

(To make ahead, store in an airtight container at room temperature for up to 1 day. Reheat in a toaster oven.)

3½ CUPS/440 G all-purpose flour

1 TBSP baking powder

2 TSP kosher salt

1 TSP baking soda

1¼ CUPS/280 G unsalted butter, cut into cubes and chilled

1½ CUPS/360 ML buttermilk

2 OZ/55 G sharp Cheddar cheese, grated

2 slices cooked bacon, chopped

2 green onions, white parts only, chopped

Heavy cream for brushing

BANANA-BUCKWHEAT GRIDDLE CAKES

There's a limited amount of space on the griddle at Brown Sugar Kitchen, so we don't offer pancakes, but I often think about how I would make them if we did. Here, I turn to buckwheat flour and flaxseed meal to give these a bit more character than pancakes made with only all-purpose flour. It also means they're gluten-free. I always have bananas around at different stages of ripeness. If you have some that are overripe, mash them before the flesh darkens and then freeze them. Thaw when ready to make this recipe.

1½ CUPS/185 G buckwheat flour
¼ CUP/35 G flaxseed meal
2 TBSP raw or turbinado sugar
2¼ TSP baking powder
½ TSP baking soda
¼ TSP kosher salt
2 OR 3 ripe bananas
2 eggs
1 CUP/240 ML plain whole-milk yogurt
1 CUP/240 ML whole milk
1 TBSP vanilla extract
3 TBSP unsalted butter, melted and cooled slightly, plus more for the griddle
Pure maple syrup for serving

In a medium bowl, whisk together the buckwheat flour, flaxseed meal, sugar, baking powder, baking soda, and salt.

In another medium bowl, mash the bananas with a wooden spoon until almost smooth. You should have about 1½ cups/340 g.

In a large bowl, whisk together the eggs, yogurt, and milk. Add the mashed bananas and vanilla and stir until thoroughly combined. Stir in the flour mixture and the melted butter until combined.

Preheat the oven to 250°F/120°C. Set a wire rack over a baking sheet. Heat a griddle or large skillet over medium-high heat and coat the surface with melted butter.

For each griddle cake, pour ¼ cup/60 ml batter onto the griddle, spacing them about 3 in/7.5 cm apart. Cook until bubbles form on top and the bottoms are golden brown, about 2 minutes. With a spatula, flip the griddle cakes and cook until the bottoms are golden brown, about 2 minutes. Transfer the griddle cakes to the rack to keep warm in the oven. Repeat with the remaining batter, placing the griddle cakes in a single layer on the rack. Serve immediately with maple syrup.

THE **BSK** BREAKFAST **TART**

When I was growing up in the '70s, quiche was a symbol of gourmet tastes and something served at fancy brunches. Today I think of it as way to combine some of the best breakfast ingredients and to highlight what's in season. In the spring you're sure to see asparagus; in the summer, tomatoes; in the fall, dark hearty greens. This version with mushrooms, spinach, and leeks is good to make all year round.

If you have a go-to pie dough recipe, definitely use it here. But if you're not inclined to make a crust from scratch, there's no shame in using a store-bought one. Puff pastry works just as well—either homemade, if you're up for it, or the frozen kind. The crust makes a light and delicate contrast to the rich custard filling.

Heat the oven to 350°F/180°C. Set the prebaked pie shell on a rimmed baking sheet next to the stove.

In a large frying pan, heat 1 tbsp oil over medium heat until shimmering. Add the mushrooms and cook until tender, about 10 minutes. Layer the cooked mushrooms in the prebaked pie shell. Heat another 1 tbsp oil in the pan, add the spinach, and cook until wilted and tender, about 5 minutes. Layer the cooked spinach on top of the mushrooms in the pie shell. Heat the remaining 1 tbsp oil in the pan, add the leeks, and cook until very tender, about 15 minutes. Layer the cooked leeks on top of the mushrooms and spinach in the pie shell. Sprinkle the Gruyère and fines herbes evenly over the top.

In a large bowl, whisk together the half-and-half, eggs, and yolks. Stir in the salt, pepper, and nutmeg. Pour the custard into the pie shell.

1 PREBAKED 9-IN/23-CM pie shell

3 TBSP olive oil

8 OZ/225 G button mushrooms, sliced

8 OZ/225 G spinach, stemmed and washed

4 leeks, white parts only, washed

2 OZ/55 G Gruyère cheese, shredded

1 TBSP fresh chopped fines herbes (equal parts parsley, tarragon, chervil, chives)

3 CUPS/720 ML half-and-half

6 eggs plus 3 egg yolks

½ TSP salt

⅛ TSP freshly ground pepper

PINCH of grated nutmeg

CONTINUED

Bake until the top is golden and the custard is just set, about 1 hour. Let cool for 10 minutes. Serve warm or at room temperature.

(To make ahead, cover tightly in plastic wrap and refrigerate for up to 2 days or freeze for up to 2 weeks. Reheat in a 350°F/180°C oven until warmed through, about 10 minutes.)

SWEET POTATO SCONES WITH BROWN SUGAR ICING

A scone has a sweeter profile and a slightly cakier texture than a biscuit. I had an idea to infuse my sweet potato obsession into a breakfast treat, so I asked our baker to come up with a recipe for sweet potato scones and she nailed it. And who wouldn't love anything topped with brown sugar icing?

To make the scones: In a wide sauté pan, melt the 1 tbsp butter over medium heat. Add the sweet potato and cook, stirring often, until it begins to soften, about 10 minutes. Add 1 tbsp of the brown sugar and cook, stirring often, until the sweet potato caramelizes, 12 to 15 minutes. Just before the sweet potato is done, stir in a pinch of salt. Refrigerate to cool completely, about 1 hour.

Preheat the oven to 425°F/220°C. Line a baking sheet with parchment paper.

In a food processor, pulse together the flour, baking powder, the remaining 2 tbsp brown sugar, ½ tsp salt, cinnamon, allspice, and nutmeg. Scatter the chilled butter cubes over the flour mixture and pulse until the mixture resembles coarse crumbs. Do not overprocess.

Transfer the flour-butter mixture to a large mixing bowl, add the currants and the chilled sweet potato, and toss to coat with the flour-butter mixture. Add the cream, gently stirring with a fork to incorporate. The dough should just barely come together. Do not overmix.

Dump the dough onto a lightly floured surface, and gently knead into a ball, taking care not to mash the sweet potato cubes. The dough will feel slightly dry. Form into an 8-in/20-cm disk and cut into eight triangles. Transfer the scones to the prepared baking sheet.

CONTINUED

SWEET POTATO SCONES

¾ CUP/170 G unsalted butter, cut into cubes and chilled, plus 1 TBSP

1 sweet potato, peeled and diced

3 TBSP firmly packed brown sugar

Kosher salt

2 CUPS/255 G all-purpose flour

1 TBSP baking powder

¼ TSP ground cinnamon

¼ TSP ground allspice

PINCH of grated nutmeg

½ CUP/70 G dried currants

¾ CUP/180 ML heavy cream, chilled

BROWN SUGAR ICING

¼ CUP/20 G powdered sugar

1 TBSP unsalted butter

¼ CUP/50 G firmly packed brown sugar

3 TBSP heavy cream

Bake until the scones are barely golden brown, 18 to 22 minutes. Let cool on the baking sheet for about 10 minutes, then transfer to a wire rack to cool completely.

To make the icing: Sift the powdered sugar into a medium bowl. In a small saucepan, combine the butter, brown sugar, and cream over medium-low heat, stirring often, until the butter is melted and the mixture is well combined. Pour the butter mixture over the powdered sugar, and whisk until smooth. Let cool completely.

When the scones are cool, set the wire rack with the scones over the baking sheet. With a small offset spatula or a table knife, spread about 1 tbsp icing on each scone. Let set for at least 15 minutes before serving.

(To make ahead, store in an airtight container for up to 2 days.)

STICKY
BUNS

Our selection of baked goods has changed over the years, depending on who's in the kitchen. But regardless of who's baking, these sticky buns have remained a constant. Because, let's be honest, you can't improve on a great sticky bun. We serve these only on Fridays, Saturdays, and Sundays, and many of our regulars show up just for these. This may be one of the more complicated baking recipes we make, but it's worth the time and effort if you're feeling ambitious. Make sure you take a picture of your finished product, as the golden brown color of these buns makes them quite photogenic! And any leftovers make an out-of-this-world bread pudding.

To make the dough: In a medium saucepan, heat ¾ cup/180 ml milk and the butter over medium heat until the butter is melted. Remove from the heat and let cool slightly.

Pour the melted butter and milk into the bowl of a standing mixer fitted with the whisk attachment. Add the granulated sugar and yeast and mix on medium speed until combined. Let stand until foamy, about 5 minutes. Add the remaining ¾ cup/180 ml milk, beaten eggs, and salt and mix on low speed until combined. Fit the mixer with the dough hook, and gradually add the flour, beating until dough is smooth and elastic, about 5 minutes.

Scrape the dough into a large oiled bowl, cover with plastic wrap, and let rise in a warm place until doubled in size, about 1 hour.

To make the sticky-bun goo: Using a clean mixer bowl and whisk attachment, cream the brown sugar and butter together on medium speed until mixture is light and fluffy, 3 to 5 minutes, scraping down the bowl at least twice. Add salt, corn syrup, honey, and water and beat until combined. Spread the goo over the bottom of a 13-by-9-in/33-by-23-cm baking pan and sprinkle evenly with pecans, if using.

DOUGH

1½ CUPS/360 ML whole milk

¾ CUP/170 G unsalted butter

¼ CUP/50 G granulated sugar

1 TBSP active dry yeast

2 eggs, beaten

1 TBSP kosher salt

5¼ CUPS/650 G all-purpose flour

STICKY-BUN GOO

¾ CUP/150 G firmly packed brown sugar

4 TBSP/55 G unsalted butter, at room temperature

½ TSP kosher salt

3 TBSP corn syrup

3 TBSP honey

1 TBSP water

1½ CUPS/170 G whole pecans (optional)

CONTINUED

To make the cinnamon sugar: In a small bowl, combine the granulated sugar and cinnamon.

Punch down the dough. On a lightly floured surface, pat into a rough rectangle. Using a lightly floured rolling pin, roll into a large rectangle about ¼ in/6 mm thick. Brush dough with the melted butter and sprinkle with cinnamon sugar. With the long side facing you, roll the dough into a log and pinch the seam to seal. Cut the log into 12 pieces, yielding 12 buns. Arrange the buns cut-side up in the prepared pan. Cover the buns with plastic wrap and let rise in a warm place until doubled in size, about 30 minutes.

Preheat the oven to 350°F/180°C.

Bake the buns until golden brown, 40 to 45 minutes. Let cool in the pan on a wire rack for 15 minutes, then invert onto a large platter. Spoon any extra goo over the buns. Serve warm.

(To make ahead, cover tightly in plastic wrap and refrigerate for up to 1 day. Unwrap and reheat on a baking sheet in a 350°F/180°C oven for about 15 minutes.)

CINNAMON SUGAR
1 CUP/200 G granulated sugar
2 TBSP ground cinnamon

6 TBSP/85 G unsalted butter, melted

VIRGINIA HAM & FRIED APPLE CROQUE-MONSIEUR

I had a student's budget and a student's diet when I went to cooking school in France. When I wasn't at school I ate a lot of baguettes, crepes, and croque-monsieurs—essentially, any combination of cheese and bread that I could think of. In this version, I've added caramelized apples to balance the salty ham and cheese and bring a little sweetness to the mix.

CARAMELIZED APPLES
1 TBSP unsalted butter

2 firm, tart apples, such as Fuji or Granny Smith, cored, peeled, and thinly sliced

1 TBSP sugar

BÉCHAMEL SAUCE
1½ TBSP unsalted butter

1½ TBSP all-purpose flour

1 CUP/240 ML whole milk, warmed

2 OZ/55 G Gruyère cheese, grated

Kosher salt

CROQUE-MONSIEUR
8 thick slices good-quality white bread such as pain de mie

4 TSP Dijon mustard

8 OZ/220 G thinly sliced ham, preferably Virginia or country ham

2 OZ/55 G Gruyère cheese, grated

To make the caramelized apples: In a large sauté pan, melt the butter over medium heat. Add the apple slices and cook just until tender, about 5 minutes. Sprinkle with the sugar and continue cooking, stirring occasionally, until the apples are glazed and caramelized, 3 to 5 minutes.

To make the béchamel sauce: In a saucepan, melt the butter over medium-low heat. Sprinkle the flour over the butter, whisking constantly, until combined. Let the mixture bubble gently for about 2 minutes, whisking all the while. Slowly pour the warmed milk into the saucepan, whisking constantly, and cook until the sauce thickens, about 3 minutes. Turn off the heat and stir in the Gruyère until melted and smooth. Season with salt.

To make the croque-monsieur: Preheat the broiler and position an oven rack at least 6 in/15 cm below the broiler element. Put the bread slices on a baking sheet and toast under the broiler, turning once, until golden brown on both sides, about 6 minutes.

Spread 4 toasted bread slices with the Dijon mustard, then layer with ham, the caramelized apples, and the Gruyère, dividing them evenly among the bread slices. Put the open-faced sandwiches on the baking sheet and broil until the cheese melts, about 3 minutes.

Top each sandwich with a slice of toasted bread, and gently press down. Slather the tops with béchamel, dividing it evenly among the sandwiches. Return the sandwiches to the broiler and cook until the béchamel is bubbly and browned, about 1 minute. Serve immediately.

THE **BSK** EGG SANDWICH

A good egg sandwich includes four essential elements—the right bread, soft scrambled eggs, juicy breakfast meat, and gooey melted cheese. At Brown Sugar Kitchen, we offer the choice of a wheat roll or a fresh croissant. I favor the latter for its over-the-top decadence, but you should choose your own favorite bread.

1 croissant or soft whole-wheat roll

2 TBSP unsalted butter, at room temperature

2 eggs, beaten

1 TBSP heavy cream

Kosher salt and freshly ground pepper

2 thin slices Monterey Jack or sharp Cheddar cheese

2 slices dry-cured ham, cooked bacon, or cooked chicken or 2 links turkey breakfast sausage

Cut the croissant in half and toast until browned. Spread cut sides with 1 tbsp butter.

In a small sauté pan, melt the remaining 1 tbsp butter over medium heat. Pour the eggs into the pan and cook, stirring constantly with a heatproof spatula or wooden spoon, until the eggs are thick and creamy and soft curds begin to form, about 1 minute. Stir in the cream and season with salt and pepper. Remove from the heat.

Set the bottom half of the croissant on a plate and top with the Monterey Jack. Spoon on the scrambled eggs, top with the ham, and cover with the top half of the roll. Serve immediately.

GRITS CAKES BENEDICT

I try to use the absolute best ingredients I can find, and that includes grits. But after trying many different kinds of fancy organic grits, I settled on using a common grocery-store brand. The consistency it yields is exactly what I'm after. Holding hollandaise sauce in a small restaurant kitchen can be a challenge—it can separate and become oily in the heat. But we still bring out this dish every now and then as a special just because it's so good. Like our breakfast potatoes in the Smoked Pork Hash (page 57), these started as a way to avoid food waste, and they ended up being a star on their own. We toast the cakes on the griddle to give them a nice crisp crust that protects the creamy centers.

To make the grits cakes: In a large, heavy-bottomed saucepan, bring the water and ½ tsp salt to a boil. Whisk in the grits, reduce to a simmer, and cook, stirring constantly, until the grits are fully cooked and thick like mush, 15 to 20 minutes.

Line a rimmed baking sheet with parchment paper. Pour the hot grits onto the prepared baking sheet; it should form a layer about ¾ in/2 cm deep. Cover with plastic wrap and let cool, then refrigerate until thoroughly chilled, at least 2 hours or up to overnight.

To make the hollandaise: In a small saucepan, combine the vinegar, bay leaf, and peppercorns and bring to a boil. Remove from heat. Let cool, then strain the vinegar, discarding the bay leaf and peppercorns.

In a small saucepan, melt the butter over medium heat. In a blender, combine the egg yolks, vinegar, and a pinch of salt and pulse to combine. With the blender running, slowly drizzle in the melted butter until the sauce has thickened. It should still be thin enough to form a pool (not a mound) when a small amount is spooned onto a cool plate. To keep warm, spoon the

CONTINUED

GRITS CAKES
5 CUPS/1.2 L water
Kosher salt
1 CUP/140 G stone-ground grits

CREOLE HOLLANDAISE
2 TBSP apple cider vinegar
1 bay leaf
3 white peppercorns
1 CUP/225 G unsalted butter
2 egg yolks
Kosher salt

8 slices deli ham or Canadian bacon (optional)
Vegetable oil for frying
½ CUP/60 G all-purpose flour
2 TSP Creole Spice Mix (page 51)
9 eggs
½ CUP/55 G plain dried bread crumbs

hollandaise into a heatproof bowl and set over a saucepan of barely simmering water, making sure the bottom of the bowl doesn't touch the water. If the sauce is too thick, add hot water, 1 tbsp at a time, to reach your desired consistency.

When the grits are cold and firm, use a 3-in/7.5-cm round cookie cutter to cut them into circles. You should have 8 grits cakes. (To make ahead, refrigerate unfried grits cakes in an airtight container for up to 3 days.)

Preheat the oven to 250°F/120°C. Place the ham, if using, in a single layer on a baking sheet to warm in the oven while frying the grits cakes.

In a large cast-iron pan, add oil to a depth of ½ in/12 mm. Heat the oil over medium heat until it reaches 350°F/180°C on an instant-read thermometer. The oil should be hot but not smoking. Line a rimmed baking sheet with paper towels and set a wire rack on top.

In a shallow dish, combine the flour and the Creole Spice Mix. In another shallow dish, lightly beat 1 egg. In a third shallow dish, pour in the bread crumbs. Set a baking sheet next to the bread crumbs.

Working in batches, dredge the grits cakes in the flour mixture, shaking off the excess. Dip the grits cakes in the beaten egg and then in the bread crumbs, lightly pressing the bread crumbs into the cakes. Put the grits cakes on the baking sheet.

CONTINUED

Fry the grits cakes a few at a time, taking care not to crowd the pan, turning once, until the cakes are golden brown, 4 to 5 minutes. Transfer to the rack over the baking sheet to keep warm in the oven. Repeat with the remaining grits cakes.

In a medium skillet, add water to a depth of about 1½ in/4 cm. Generously salt the water and bring to a simmer over medium-high heat. Carefully break 4 eggs, one at a time, and slip into the water, taking care not to crowd the pan. Cook until the whites are set and the yolks are still runny, about 3 minutes. With a slotted spoon, transfer the eggs to a kitchen towel to drain. Repeat with the remaining 4 eggs.

Place 2 grits cakes on each plate. Top each grits cake with 1 slice of ham, if using, and 1 poached egg. Spoon the Creole Hollandaise over the eggs. Serve immediately.

(To reheat fried cakes, place them on an ungreased baking sheet in a 350°F/180°C oven and bake for 10 to 15 minutes.)

CREOLE **SPICE MIX**

In a small bowl, stir together the salt, herbes de Provence, cumin, cayenne, black pepper, and paprika until thoroughly combined. (To make ahead, store in an airtight container for up to 6 months.)

3 TBSP kosher salt

3 TBSP herbes de Provence

3 TBSP ground cumin

⅓ CUP/45 G cayenne pepper

¼ CUP/30 G freshly ground black pepper

¼ CUP/30 G sweet paprika

CREOLE
SHRIMP & GRITS

Creole food is city food, slightly more rarefied than its rustic Cajun cousin, with roots that reach back to Louisiana's French colonists. You can certainly see the French connection in this recipe—the base of the sauce is a *brunoise* (finely diced vegetables), the sauce itself is a reduction that's mounted with butter, and the shrimp is cooked with a quick sauté . . . *très française, n'est pas?* One not-so-French element here is the hefeweizen I use in the Creole sauce. Its light, citrusy flavor intensifies as it reduces and helps cut some of the richness of this luxurious dish. This dish has quite a following at BSK; it's a popular item on our breakfast and brunch menu, but it's equally at home on the dinner table.

In a large sauté pan, heat the oil over medium heat until shimmering. Add the green and red bell peppers, green onions, garlic, and the Creole Spice Mix, and cook until the vegetables are softened, about 5 minutes. Add the shrimp and sear just until opaque, turning once, about 2 minutes. Stir in the Creole Sauce, cream, and butter, and bring to a simmer. Add the spinach, a handful at a time, stirring to wilt and coat with sauce. Once all the spinach has been added, remove the pan from the heat and stir in the lemon juice. Serve immediately over the grits.

2 TBSP vegetable oil

¼ CUP/40 G diced green bell pepper

¼ CUP/40 G diced red bell pepper

3 green onions, white and green parts, thinly sliced

2 garlic cloves, minced

2 TSP Creole Spice Mix (page 51)

1½ LB/680 G medium shrimp, peeled and deveined

¾ CUP/180 ML Creole Sauce (page 54)

¼ CUP/60 ML heavy cream

2 TBSP unsalted butter

5 OZ/140 G baby spinach leaves

2 TSP fresh lemon juice

White Cheddar Grits (page 54) for serving

CREOLE **SAUCE**

1 TBSP unsalted butter

2 green onions, white parts only, chopped

1 TSP minced garlic

ONE 12-oz/360-ml bottle wheat beer, such as hefeweizen

¾ CUP/180 ML Worcestershire sauce

In a medium saucepan, melt the butter over low heat. Add the green onions and garlic, and cook until softened, about 5 minutes. Add the beer and Worcestershire sauce and increase the heat to medium-high. Bring to a boil, reduce to a simmer, and cook until thick and syrupy and reduced to about 1 cup/240 ml, 15 to 20 minutes. Remove from heat and let cool. (To make ahead, refrigerate sauce in an airtight container for up to 1 week.)

SERVES 4

WHITE CHEDDAR **GRITS**

2¾ CUPS/660 ML water

⅔ CUP/95 G quick-cooking grits

2 TBSP heavy cream

2 TBSP unsalted butter

4 OZ/115 G sharp white Cheddar cheese, grated

1½ TSP kosher salt

PINCH of white pepper

In a medium saucepan, bring the water to a boil. Whisk in the grits, reduce to a simmer, and cook, stirring constantly, until the grits are fully cooked and thick like mush, about 4 minutes. Stir in the cream, butter, cheese, salt, and white pepper.

Cover and keep warm over very low heat until serving.

SWEET POTATO-KALE HASH

When I was in high school and college, I dabbled with being a vegetarian, by which I mean that I ate a lot of pasta and every now and then I would sneak a piece of chicken. But then I moved to New York City, fell in love with restaurants and cooking, and my vegetarian diet fell by the wayside. This dish is one to honor my vegetarian past and my vegetarian friends and customers today. Of course, many meat eaters enjoy it too.

In a large pot, cover the sweet potatoes with cold water. Season the water generously with salt and bring to a boil. Reduce to a simmer and cook until the sweet potatoes are slightly softened, about 5 minutes. Drain.

In a medium sauté pan, heat the oil over medium heat until shimmering. Add the onion and cook until tender and translucent, about 5 minutes. Add the red and yellow bell peppers, kale, and green onions, and cook, stirring occasionally, until the bell peppers are softened, about 5 minutes. Add the sweet potatoes and parsley and season with salt and pepper. Increase the heat to medium-high and allow the vegetables to caramelize, stirring occasionally, until well browned and crisp in places, about 10 minutes.

Serve immediately.

(To make ahead, refrigerate the cooked hash in an airtight container for up to 2 days. Reheat in a sauté pan over medium heat with 1 tbsp vegetable oil.)

2 LB/910 G red-skinned sweet potatoes, peeled and cut into ½-in/12-mm dice

Kosher salt

2 TBSP vegetable oil

1 yellow onion, cut into ¼-in/6-mm slices

¼ CUP/40 G diced red bell pepper

¼ CUP/40 G diced yellow bell pepper

1 bunch kale, stemmed and cut into ¼-in/6-mm strips

2 green onions, white and green parts, chopped

1 TBSP chopped fresh parsley

Freshly ground pepper

SMOKED PORK HASH

Like a musician, I love a great collaboration. This dish came at the suggestion of my friend and colleague Amey Shaw, who was helping in our kitchen and noticed that we often had leftover jerked baby back ribs and breakfast potatoes that we couldn't serve the next day. It was her brilliant idea to combine the two, and this "use it up" dish has since become a star player on our menu. It started as a special that kept selling out. Now we fire up extra ribs and potatoes just to make this hash. It also makes an excellent bed for a freshly poached egg.

In a large pot, cover the potatoes with cold water. Season the water generously with salt and bring to a boil. Reduce to a simmer and cook until the potatoes are slightly softened, about 5 minutes. Drain.

In a medium sauté pan, heat the oil over medium heat until shimmering. Add the onion and cook until tender and translucent, about 5 minutes. Add the red and yellow bell peppers, spinach, and green onions, and cook, stirring occasionally, until the bell peppers are softened, about 5 minutes. Add the potatoes, pork, and parsley, and season with salt and pepper. Stir in the cream and hot pepper sauce to taste (if using). Increase the heat to medium-high and allow the vegetables to caramelize, stirring occasionally, until the hash is well browned and crisp in places, about 10 minutes.

To serve, sprinkle with parsley and top with poached eggs, if you like.

(To make ahead, refrigerate the cooked hash in an airtight container for up to 3 days. Reheat in a sauté pan over medium heat with 1 tbsp vegetable oil.)

1 LB/455 G Yukon Gold potatoes, cut into ½-in/12-mm dice

Kosher salt

2 TBSP vegetable oil

1 yellow onion, cut into ¼-in/6-mm slices

¼ CUP/40 G diced red bell pepper

¼ CUP/40 G diced yellow bell pepper

1 LB/455 G spinach, stemmed, washed, and cut into ¼-in/6-mm strips

2 green onions, white and green parts, chopped

9 OZ/255 G diced cooked smoked pork (leftover short ribs are delicious)

1 TBSP chopped fresh parsley, plus more for garnish

Freshly ground pepper

3 TBSP heavy cream

Hot pepper sauce (optional)

8 eggs, poached (see page 50; optional)

BSK BREAKFAST
POTATOES

On Saturday mornings my dad would make home fries with frozen, cut potatoes, bell peppers, onions, and "secret spices." I loved to smell them cooking while I was still in bed. At the restaurant, I use fresh Yukon Gold potatoes because they have a naturally buttery flavor, and a mix of garlic, cayenne, and paprika that gives the dish a real kick. The potatoes are soft on the inside and crisp on the outside and the caramelized onions add a touch of sweetness that balances the heat.

¼ CUP/60 ML canola oil, plus 2 TBSP

1 yellow onion, cut into ¼-in/6-mm slices

¼ CUP/60 ML water

2 LB/910 G Yukon Gold potatoes, cut into 1-in/2.5-cm pieces

2½ TSP kosher salt

1½ TSP dried thyme

1 TSP dried tarragon

¼ TSP onion powder

¼ TSP garlic powder

¼ TSP cayenne pepper

¼ TSP sweet paprika

¼ TSP freshly ground black pepper

In a large sauté pan, heat the ¼ cup/60 ml oil over medium heat until shimmering and very hot but not smoking. Add the onion and cook, without stirring, until deep brown on the bottom, but not burned, about 5 minutes. Add the water and stir the onion. Continue cooking, stirring occasionally, until the onions are softened and evenly caramelized, about 10 minutes more.

Meanwhile, in another large sauté pan or cast-iron skillet, heat the remaining 2 tbsp oil over medium-high heat until shimmering. Add the potatoes and salt, and cook, without stirring, until the potatoes begin to brown, about 5 minutes. Stir the potatoes and add the thyme, tarragon, onion powder, garlic powder, cayenne, paprika, and black pepper. Continue to cook, stirring occasionally, until the potatoes are browned all over and cooked through, about 15 minutes. Stir in the caramelized onions. Serve immediately.

CHICKEN-APPLE SAUSAGE CORNBREAD PUDDING

This is a dish I like to make when I have guests for breakfast. I can assemble this the night before or even days ahead and refrigerate or freeze it, then pop it in the oven just before everyone is ready to eat. You can use turkey or pork sausage, or make it vegetarian by leaving out the meat and adding some broccoli.

1 TBSP unsalted butter, plus more for the baking dish

½ yellow onion, diced

2 stalks celery, diced

½ yellow or red bell pepper, diced

6 OZ/170 G chicken-apple sausages, diced, precooked

1 TSP Creole Spice Mix (page 51)

4 CUPS/455 G cubed Buttermilk Cornbread (page 106)

4 eggs

2 egg yolks

1½ CUPS/350 ML whole milk

¾ CUP/175 ML heavy cream

Kosher salt

Preheat the oven to 350°F/180°C. Butter an 8-by-8-in/20-by-20-cm Pyrex baking dish.

In a large sauté pan, melt the butter over medium heat. Add the onion and cook until tender and translucent, about 5 minutes. Add the celery and bell pepper and cook until softened, about 3 minutes more. Add the sausage and cook, stirring occasionally, until the sausage is heated through and begins to brown. Stir in the Creole Spice Mix, and remove from the heat.

Add the cornbread to the pan and toss until combined. Spoon the cornbread and vegetable mixture into the prepared baking dish.

In a large bowl, whisk together the eggs, yolks, milk, cream, and ½ tsp salt. Pour over the cornbread mixture. Cover the baking dish with aluminum foil. (To make ahead, refrigerate for up to 2 days or freeze for up to 1 month.)

Bake, covered, for 30 minutes, or 45 minutes if baking frozen. Uncover and bake for 20 to 30 minutes more, until the pudding is browned and puffed and a knife inserted in the center comes out clean. Let cool for 10 minutes before serving. Cut the bread pudding into squares and serve warm.

NUTTY GRANOLA

Brown Sugar Kitchen is best known for hot breakfasts, like cornmeal waffles and smoked pork hash, but our granola has a following of its own. Making granola at home is easier than you think, and you can customize it to your taste: Use more of your favorite nut and leave out another one. Add dried blueberries, cranberries, or currants. As long as you keep the ratio of nuts to dried fruit the same, your granola will be delicious.

Preheat the oven to 325°F/165°C. Line a rimmed baking sheet with parchment paper.

In a small saucepan, combine the coconut oil, butter, agave syrup, brown sugar, and salt, and bring to a simmer. Remove from the heat and stir in the vanilla, cinnamon, and ginger.

In a large bowl, combine the oats, almonds, coconut, pumpkin seeds, pine nuts, pistachios, and pecans. Pour the warm oil–agave syrup mixture over the oat-nut mixture and stir until the dry ingredients are evenly coated.

Spread the granola in a single layer on the prepared baking sheet. Bake, stirring several times, until the granola is evenly browned, about 25 minutes.

Let cool completely on the baking sheet. Serve at room temperature with yogurt and fruit, if you like.

(To make ahead, store in an airtight container for up to 1 month.)

¼ CUP/60 ML coconut oil

4 TBSP/55 G unsalted butter

¾ CUP/180 ML agave syrup

½ CUP/100 G firmly packed brown sugar

1 TSP kosher salt

1 TSP vanilla extract

½ TSP ground cinnamon

¼ TSP ground ginger

5 CUPS/430 G rolled oats

1½ CUPS/170 G sliced blanched almonds

1 CUP/90 G unsweetened flaked coconut

¾ CUP/80 G pumpkin seeds

½ CUP/55 G pine nuts

½ CUP/55 G shelled pistachios

½ CUP/55 G pecan pieces

Yogurt for serving (optional)

Fresh fruit for serving (optional)

OAKLAND LOCAL

Running a restaurant in a region with such a rich agricultural heritage and with so many small-scale food producers means that it's easy for us to find high-quality local ingredients and build relationships with the people who make them. I'm particularly proud of the fact that we're able to get many of our products from people working right here in West Oakland.

Brown Sugar Kitchen had been open for just about six months when Alex Roberts and Andrew Green from **RoastCo** (their roastery is less than a mile from the restaurant) came to talk to me about their custom blends. We decided to work together to develop a house coffee based on the qualities I like best in my morning cup. I knew I wanted something dark, but not too dark, with rich chocolate notes. With their help, I decided on a medium roast that combines seasonal coffees from several major growing regions.

Alex and Andrew have also played an important role in educating our servers and baristas, making sure they understand the nuances of brewing great coffee. We get weekly deliveries of fresh roasted beans and grind them just before brewing. That makes an enormous difference in flavor. Bags of Brown Sugar Kitchen blend beans are sold in a handful of local markets as well as through the RoastCo website, so fans of our coffee can also enjoy it at home.

West Oakland, with its wide trucking thoroughfares and huge concrete warehouses, is not a place that one expects to find a farm, but in fact, many of the empty lots here have been taken over by intrepid urban farmers. It's not at all unusual to see chickens scratching behind a chain-link fence and tomato plants growing in corner lots. **City Slicker Farms**, one of the Bay Area's most respected urban agriculture programs,

is here. They've taken over several vacant lots in the neighborhood and turned them into thriving local farms, some with their own farmers' markets. They also work in backyard gardens, teaching West Oakland residents how to grow their own food—an effort that's far more empowering than simply passing out bags of groceries.

Though they don't grow enough vegetables to supply our restaurant, I sit on the advisory board and support them with fundraising events. Once a week, someone from the farm comes by the restaurant on a pedal-powered vehicle to pick up food scraps to use for compost and chicken feed back at the farm. It's a way for us to complete the cycle for food at the restaurant and helps ensure that nothing from our kitchen is ever wasted. Our involvement with City Slicker Farms is a way for Brown Sugar Kitchen to give back to the community that does so much to support us.

When most people think of California wines, they picture the large-production wineries in Napa and the beautiful vineyards that wind their way over the Sonoma hillsides. It's also true that's there's some excellent wine made right here in Oakland. Some of our favorites come from **Urban Legend**. Run by Marilee and Steve Shaffer, veterans of the tech world with a strong creative bent, the winery is in a warehouse on the waterfront in Oakland's Ironworks District near Jack London Square.

It's the smallest of small businesses. Marilee is the winemaker, Steve focuses on marketing; she does the accounting, he designed the website and built the tasting counter. Their wines are particularly food-friendly. I'm a big fan of their grenache blend. It reminds me of wines I drank in the south of France. We also feature their sauvignon blanc, which is nice and crisp and goes well with the spicier dishes on our menu.

CHAPTER 2
SNACKS
& SALADS

These are the bits and bites I gravitate to when I want something to eat, but am not quite hungry enough for a meal, dishes I put out when I'm having friends over for drinks or a casual meal. Fancy doesn't figure in much at those gatherings, but flavor is always at the front of my mind.

I do love a good cocktail party with an ample offering of finger foods. There's much to admire in a chef who can create a balance of flavors in a single, small mouthful. Here you'll find my own versions of cocktail food, like my baked chicken wings and crisp fried okra, known to convert the most ardent okra-phobes. You'll see, too, that I like to tinker with European classics, like gougères, Burgundian cheese puffs, that I've spiked with andouille, one of my favorite Cajun sausages.

I'm especially sensitive to seasonality, and few dishes better illustrate the importance of balancing ingredients and textures than salads do. One, like the Little Gems with shrimp and Thousand Island dressing, is a dance between the crisp heads of lettuce, sweet, briny shrimp, and that luscious, thick dressing. Too much lettuce, too few shrimp, and a heavy hand with the Thousand Island, and the dish is a mess. But bring it all together in just the right measure, and it's an elegant, irresistible addition to a meal.

I've chosen this collection for you as many are on our menu and we run a composed salad special that changes weekly. Here are some of my favorites.

SPICY BAKED WINGS

The search for great chicken wings is over. We serve these at our sister restaurant, B-Side BBQ, and it's one of those dishes that always get a big reaction (like Phil jumping up and down). Great wings make people happy. These are perfect for game night or for no particular reason at all. The beauty is that they're baked and gluten-free and you can adjust the seasoning to your taste. Wings have become so popular that markets now sell them trimmed and ready to use, often labeled "party wings."

Vegetable oil for the baking sheets

4 LB/1.8 KG whole chicken wings or 3 LB/1.4 KG trimmed

1 TBSP dry mustard

1 TSP ground ginger

1 TSP kosher salt

1 TSP freshly ground black pepper

¼ TSP ground allspice

¼ TSP cayenne pepper

4 TBSP/55 G unsalted butter

4 large garlic cloves, minced

1 TBSP sauce from canned chipotle chiles in adobo

2 TSP Tabasco sauce

2 TBSP Crystal hot sauce

⅔ CUP/225 G honey

Preheat the oven to 425°F/220°C. Line two large rimmed baking sheets with aluminum foil and lightly coat with oil.

If using whole wings, separate the sections of chicken wings at the joints, discarding or saving the wing tip portion for another use.

In a large bowl, combine the mustard, ginger, salt, black pepper, allspice, and cayenne.

In a small saucepan, melt the butter over medium heat. Add the garlic and cook until garlic is fragrant and softened, about 2 minutes. Stir in the chipotle sauce, Tabasco sauce, Crystal hot sauce, and honey, and bring to a simmer, about 5 minutes. (To make ahead, refrigerate in an airtight container for up to 2 days.)

Pour about half of the sauce into the large bowl with the dry spices, and stir until combined. (Reserve the remaining sauce in the pan.) Add the chicken wings and toss until the wings are evenly coated with the sauce.

Spread the chicken wings in a single layer on the prepared baking sheets. Be sure that the chicken wings have enough space between them to brown well on all sides. Bake for 25 minutes, then flip the wings, and bake for 25 minutes more, until the wings are cooked through and well browned.

Reheat the remaining sauce over medium heat until bubbling, 4 to 5 minutes. Transfer to a large bowl. Add the hot wings to the bowl and toss until the wings are well coated with the sauce. Serve warm or at room temperature.

(To make ahead, refrigerate the baked wings for up to 3 days. To reheat, spread the chilled wings on a foil-lined baking sheet and bake in a 300°F/150°C oven for about 10 minutes.)

ANDOUILLE GOUGÈRES

Gougères are sophisticated cheese puffs and are the appetizer of choice in Burgundy, France, where I went to cooking school. They're made from a base known as pâté à choux, a very elementary dough and one of the first I learned to make. Don't be intimidated by the fancy French name. Pâté à choux is easy to master and versatile too. It's the foundation for many famous pastries including éclairs and cream puffs, and as you see here, it also comes in handy for savory treats. For this Cajun-inspired version, I decided that a crumble of spicy andouille might just put them over the top.

1 CUP/240 ML water

½ CUP/115 G unsalted butter

Kosher salt

1 CUP/125 G all-purpose flour

5 eggs

2½ OZ/70 G Gruyère cheese, grated

4 OZ/115 G andouille sausage, chopped

Preheat the oven to 425°F/220°C. Line two baking sheets with parchment paper.

In a large saucepan, combine the water, butter, and ½ tsp salt. Bring to a boil over medium-high heat. When the butter has melted, add the flour all at once, stirring vigorously with a wooden spoon. Reduce the heat to medium, and keep stirring until the mixture has formed a smooth, thick paste and pulls away from the sides of the pan, about 3 minutes. Transfer to the bowl of a stand mixer fitted with the paddle attachment or to a large heatproof bowl.

If using a stand mixer, add 4 eggs, one at a time, mixing on low speed until the egg is incorporated and the dough is smooth before adding the next egg. (If mixing by hand, add 4 eggs, one at a time, stirring with a wooden spoon until the egg is incorporated and the dough is smooth before adding the next egg.) The mixture should be very thick, smooth, and shiny. Stir in the Gruyère and andouille. (To make ahead, cover the bowl tightly with plastic wrap and refrigerate for up to 1 day.)

Use a tablespoon to drop the dough into 1-in/2.5-cm rounds about 1½ in/4 cm apart on the prepared baking sheets. You should have about 2 dozen gougères.

CONTINUED

In a small bowl, whisk the remaining egg with a pinch of salt to make an egg wash. Brush the top of each gougère with the egg wash.

Bake for 15 minutes. Reduce the oven to 375°F/190°C, rotate the baking sheets, and continue baking until the gougères are puffed and nicely browned, about 15 minutes more.

Serve warm or at room temperature.

(Baked gougères can be frozen for up to 1 month. Reheat in a 350°F/180°C oven for 8 to 10 minutes.)

CORNMEAL-COATED OKRA BITES

This is an okra dish that handily converts haters of this often maligned vegetable. Dredged in a slightly spicy cornmeal mixture and quickly fried, these little nuggets are deliciously crisp and never have that bit of sliminess that turns some folks off. Refrigerating the okra slices before frying is an extra bit of anti-slime insurance.

Trim the okra, cut into ¼-in/6-mm slices, and refrigerate for about 30 minutes. Preheat the oven to 250°F/120°C.

In a large cast-iron frying pan at least 4 in/10 cm deep, add oil to a depth of 2 in/5 cm. Heat the oil over medium heat until it reaches 350°F/180°C on an instant-read thermometer. The oil should be hot but not smoking. Line a rimmed baking sheet with paper towels and set a wire rack on top.

In a shallow dish, combine the cornmeal, flour, and the Creole Spice Mix. In another shallow dish, pour the buttermilk.

A handful at a time, add the chilled okra slices to the buttermilk, tossing gently with a fork until they are well coated. Using a slotted spoon and letting any excess buttermilk drip back into the bowl, transfer the okra to the cornmeal mixture. Toss the okra pieces in the cornmeal mixture until they are well coated.

Fry the okra, a few large spoonfuls at a time, taking care not to crowd the pan and turning occasionally, until crisp and lightly browned, 3 to 5 minutes. Transfer to the rack over the baking sheet and keep warm in the oven. Repeat with the remaining okra.

Season with salt and pepper. Serve immediately.

2 LB/910 G okra
Vegetable oil for frying
1 CUP/140 G cornmeal
½ CUP/60 G all-purpose flour
1 TBSP Creole Spice Mix [page 51]
1 CUP/240 ML buttermilk
Kosher salt
Freshly ground pepper

MIXED GREENS WITH ROASTED TOMATO & THYME VINAIGRETTE

This is a perfect salad for brunch; just add a poached or soft-boiled egg. The recipe for the roasted tomato and thyme vinaigrette makes more than you need for this salad, but you'll want to have plenty of it on hand for other uses. It makes a delicious sauce for grilled fish and is terrific drizzled on a steak.

ROASTED TOMATO & THYME VINAIGRETTE

1 ripe Roma tomato, peeled, halved, and seeded

¼ CUP/60 ML extra-virgin olive oil, plus more for drizzling

Kosher salt and freshly ground pepper

2 TSP minced shallots

½ TSP fresh thyme leaves

1 TBSP red wine vinegar

CROUTONS

3 OZ/85 G Buttermilk Cornbread (page 106), cut into 1-in/2.5-cm cubes

Extra-virgin olive oil for drizzling

Kosher salt

12 OZ/340 G mixed greens (such as baby romaine, frisée, oak leaf lettuce, baby spinach, and arugula), torn into bite-size pieces

2 strips cooked bacon, crumbled

To make the vinaigrette: Preheat the oven to 350°F/180°C. In a small baking dish, add the tomato, drizzle with oil, and season with salt and pepper. Bake until the tomato is roasted and the juices are lightly caramelized, 15 to 20 minutes. Let cool to room temperature. Do not turn off the oven.

In a blender or food processor, combine the tomato, ¼ cup/ 60 ml oil, shallots, thyme, and vinegar, and process until blended but still slightly chunky. Season with salt and pepper. (To make ahead, refrigerate in an airtight container for up to 3 days.)

To make the croutons: On a baking sheet, spread the cornbread in a single layer and drizzle with oil and sprinkle with salt. Bake, turning the croutons over once or twice, until they are slightly browned, about 15 minutes.

In a large salad bowl, toss the mixed greens, bacon, and croutons with about ¼ cup/60 ml of the vinaigrette. Serve immediately.

SPINACH SALAD WITH ROASTED APPLE DRESSING, TOASTED PECANS & GOAT CHEESE

A great salad must be perfectly dressed, with dressing lightly coating each leaf. None of this drizzle-over-the-top stuff. I like to mix frisée with spinach to add to the color and texture. The addition of some protein—roast chicken, roast turkey, or smoked trout—turns this salad into a satisfying main course.

To make the dressing: In a small saucepan, combine the apple, shallot, garlic, thyme, and apple cider and cook over medium heat until the apple is tender and most of the liquid has cooked down, about 10 minutes. In a blender or food processor, combine the cooked apple mixture with the vinegar and process until smooth. With the blender running, drizzle in the canola and olive oils and process until smooth. Season with salt and pepper. (To make ahead, refrigerate in an airtight container for up to 3 days.)

In a large salad bowl, combine the spinach, frisee, apple, chèvre, and pecans. Season with salt and pepper and toss with 2 tbsp of the dressing. Serve immediately.

Toasting nuts or spices

Heat a dry frying pan over medium heat. Add the nuts or spices and toast, stirring occasionally just until fragrant.

ROASTED APPLE DRESSING

1 firm, tart apple, such as Honeycrisp or Fuji, cored, peeled, and chopped into ½-in/12-mm pieces

1 large shallot, minced

1 garlic clove, minced

1 TBSP fresh thyme leaves

1 CUP/240 ML apple cider or good-quality apple juice

¼ CUP/60 ML apple cider vinegar

¼ CUP/60 ML canola oil

¼ CUP/60 ML extra-virgin olive oil

Kosher salt and freshly ground pepper

6 OZ/170 G baby spinach leaves

1 generous handful frisee

1 firm, tart apple, such as Honeycrisp or Fuji, cored, peeled, and thinly sliced

3 OZ/85 G chèvre or other soft goat cheese, crumbled

½ CUP/55 G pecan pieces, toasted and chopped

Kosher salt and freshly ground pepper

ROMAINE SALAD WITH SPRING VEGETABLES & CUCUMBER-BUTTERMILK DRESSING

Romaine demands a dressing that clings. Like iceberg, it contains a lot of water and needs a flavorful dressing to boost its appeal. This dressing is subtle, but nicely balanced with the herbs and cucumber flavors. Buttermilk gives it the creamy quality of a rich dressing without the heaviness of one based on mayonnaise or cream.

To make the dressing: In a blender or food processor, combine the cucumber, buttermilk, sour cream, shallot, chives, parsley, honey, lemon juice, paprika, and cayenne, and process until smooth. Season with salt and pepper. (To make ahead, refrigerate in an airtight container for up to 1 week.)

In a large pot of boiling salted water, cook the snap peas just until tender, about 5 minutes. Drain and let cool to room temperature. Cut into 1/2-in/12-mm pieces.

Using a vegetable peeler, shave the radishes, carrot, and asparagus spears into thin slices or thinly slice with a knife. Break apart the romaine head and tear the leaves into large pieces.

Put the lettuce on a large serving platter, and scatter the shaved vegetables and the snap peas on top. Add the cucumber-buttermilk dressing and gently combine. Serve immediately.

CUCUMBER-BUTTERMILK DRESSING

1 small cucumber, peeled, seeded, and grated
1/4 CUP/60 ML buttermilk
1 TBSP sour cream
1 TBSP minced shallot
1 TSP chopped fresh chives
1 TSP chopped fresh parsley
1/2 TSP honey or agave syrup
1 TSP fresh lemon juice
1/4 TSP sweet paprika
1/8 TSP cayenne pepper
Kosher salt and freshly ground black pepper

4 OZ/115 G sugar snap peas, trimmed and tough strings removed
4 radishes
1 carrot, peeled
2 thick spears asparagus, tough ends snapped off
1 large head romaine lettuce

BLACK-EYED PEA SALAD

I'm not sure why, but sometimes it takes a bit of convincing to get people to try black-eyed peas. Somewhere along the way, these beans developed a reputation as muddy tasting and mushy. Well, not my black-eyed peas and not this recipe. The key is to not overcook the beans and to strain them out of their cooking liquid once they're done. Then their flavor is delicate and earthy and the texture just right to the bite. I love them tossed in this simple vinaigrette with a few other vegetables and lots of fresh herbs.

In a large bowl, cover the black-eyed peas with 2 to 3 in/5 to 7.5 cm of cold water and let soak overnight.

Drain and rinse the beans, and transfer them to a large soup pot. Add enough fresh cold water to cover the beans by about 3 in/ 7.5 cm. Bring to a boil, reduce to a simmer, and cook until peas are tender, 30 to 40 minutes. Stir in the salt and allow the beans to rest for 5 minutes to absorb the salt. Drain the peas and let cool to room temperature.

Transfer the peas to a large bowl. Add the onion, bell peppers, jalapeño, parsley, and cilantro. Stir to combine. Season with salt and pepper.

In a small bowl, whisk together the vinegar and oil. Add this dressing to salad and toss before serving. Serve at room temperature.

(To make ahead, refrigerate the salad for up to 3 days. Bring to room temperature before serving.)

3 CUPS/600 G dried black-eyed peas, picked over and rinsed

1 TBSP Kosher salt

½ white onion, diced

½ CUP/120 G diced roasted red bell peppers, freshly roasted or jarred

1 TBSP minced jalapeño chile

2 TSP chopped fresh parsley

2 TSP chopped fresh cilantro

Salt and freshly ground pepper

3 TBSP red wine vinegar

3 TSP olive oil

LITTLE GEMS & SHRIMP SALAD WITH THOUSAND ISLAND DRESSING

If you can't find Little Gems, substitute romaine lettuce. You want a hearty green that can hold this thick, chunky dressing. I like the addition of shrimp in this salad, which turns it into a main course. At the restaurant, our smoker is always going, so we cook the shrimp in it to give the salad another layer of flavor. You can do the same at home, with a gas or charcoal grill, if you like. Many of us grew up with the bottled Thousand Island dressing, which seems quite mundane until you make it from scratch—then it becomes divine.

THOUSAND ISLAND DRESSING

1 egg

½ CUP/115 G mayonnaise

2 TBSP chili sauce, such as Heinz

1 TBSP sweet pickle relish

1 green onion, white part only, chopped

1 TBSP finely chopped pimento-stuffed green olives

1 TSP chopped fresh parsley

⅛ TSP cayenne pepper

⅛ TSP smoked paprika

⅛ TSP garlic powder

Kosher salt and freshly ground pepper

8 OZ/225 G medium shrimp

4 HEADS Little Gems lettuce, torn into bite-size pieces

To make the dressing: In a small saucepan, cover the egg with cold water and bring to a boil. Once the water boils, cover the pan, turn off the heat, and let stand for 7 minutes. Drain and rinse the egg with cold water. Peel and chop the egg.

In a small bowl, combine the chopped egg, mayonnaise, chili sauce, pickle relish, green onion, olives, parsley, cayenne, paprika, and garlic powder. Season with salt and pepper. (To make ahead, refrigerate in an airtight container for up to 3 days.)

In a large pot of boiling salted water, cook the shrimp until opaque, about 2 minutes. Drain and let cool. Peel the shrimp and remove the dark vein that runs down the back.

Arrange the lettuce on a chilled serving platter and top with the shrimp. Pour the dressing over all. Serve immediately.

PICNIC-WORTHY
POTATO SALAD

When I was growing up, the ingredients for the best potato salad were the subject of ongoing debate. Eggs or no eggs? Sweet pickle relish or dill? White or green onions? Mustard and mayo? Firm cooked potatoes or mashed to a purée? Over the years I've tried them all and come up with this version, which gets my vote as the absolute best. I love this potato salad at room temperature, but it can be refrigerated to let the flavors meld for several hours or up to overnight before serving.

In a large saucepan, cover the potatoes with cold water. Season the water generously with salt and bring to a boil. Reduce to a simmer and cook until the potatoes are tender but not falling apart, about 15 minutes. Drain and transfer to a large bowl.

In a small saucepan, cover the eggs with cold water and bring to a boil. Once the water boils, cover the pan, turn off the heat, and let stand for 7 minutes. Drain and rinse the eggs with cold water. Peel and dice the eggs.

In a small bowl, combine the eggs, green onions, celery, mayonnaise, garlic, lemon juice, the Dijon and whole-grain mustards, paprika, vinegar, salt, and pepper. Gently fold into the warm potatoes; it is important to dress the potatoes while they're warm so they soak up the flavors. Serve immediately. Or refrigerate for up to 12 hours to let the flavors meld; bring to room temperature before serving.

1½ LB/680 G Yukon Gold potatoes, peeled and cut into 1-in/2.5-cm pieces

2 eggs

3 green onions, white and green parts, chopped

1 stalk celery, diced

¾ CUP/170 G mayonnaise

3 garlic cloves, minced

Juice of 1 lemon

1 TBSP Dijon mustard

1 TBSP whole-grain mustard

¼ TSP sweet paprika

2 TBSP apple cider vinegar

2 TSP kosher salt

¼ TSP freshly ground pepper

SPICY GREEN COLESLAW

This coleslaw is one of my favorite side dishes—I eat it several times a week. It's light and refreshing, without any of the heaviness of mayonnaise. Its slight acidic flavor makes it a great partner for richer, meaty dishes like our BBQ Pulled-Pork Sandwich (see page 123) or Jerk Baby Back Ribs with Pineapple Salsa (see page 138). The green cabbage doesn't bleed like red cabbage does, so you can dress it several hours before serving—ideal for taking on a picnic.

VINAIGRETTE

¼ CUP/60 ML red wine vinegar

1 red onion, cut into rough chunks

3 garlic cloves, peeled

2 jalapeño chiles, coarsely chopped

1½ CUPS/360 ML canola oil

½ TSP kosher salt

1 small green cabbage, cut into ⅛-in/4-mm shreds

1 red onion, cut into ⅛-in/4-mm slices

2 TBSP chopped fresh cilantro

½ TSP celery seeds

¼ TSP kosher salt

¼ TSP freshly ground pepper

To make the vinaigrette: In a blender or food processor, combine the vinegar, onion, garlic, jalapeño, oil, and salt and process until smooth. (To make ahead, refrigerate in an airtight container for up to 3 days.)

In a large salad bowl, combine the cabbage, onion, and cilantro. Sprinkle with the celery seeds, salt, and pepper and mix thoroughly. Add the vinaigrette and toss to thoroughly coat. Serve immediately. (To make ahead, refrigerate the salad for up to 2 days. Bring to room temperature before serving.)

LA CHICA MALA
AKA CYNTHIA CURIEL

DOG WALKER AND SKATER FOR THE B.AY A.REA D.ERBY GIRLS

Lives: Dogtown, West Oakland, since 2012

Regular order: Eggs and grits, and an iced soy latte with vanilla syrup

I got to know the neighborhood in 2010, when I started coming here for roller derby practice. (The rink is directly across the street from Brown Sugar Kitchen.) I liked what I saw and ended up moving here from San Francisco in 2012. There are a lot of families buying homes and a huge number of artists living here. It's a very diverse community. There are fancy, fancy lofts that the commuters live in, and then there's the low-income housing. Then I see people like me. It's an interesting place. It's not perfect, but it's sunny and affordable. I can't emphasize enough how much I love my house and my yard, and the sunshine. I rarely have time for a sit-down breakfast, but I come to Brown Sugar Kitchen every morning for coffee. I used to bring a jar of vanilla syrup to add to it. It's just something I have to have, but then Tanya noticed what I was doing and she started making vanilla syrup just for me. I'm sure I'm the only one who ever orders it, but it's always here for me.

THE ACCIDENTAL RESTAURATEUR

My husband, Phil Surkis, never intended to make Brown Sugar Kitchen his career. I told him I wanted to open a restaurant on our first date (we dined on barbecue and Champagne, by the way), and he didn't back down.

As the opening of Brown Sugar Kitchen approached, Phil became what he likes to call "the accidental restaurateur," taking on what amounted to be almost a second full-time job in addition to his day job as a workers'-compensation claims adjuster. He quickly learned that when you marry a chef, the restaurant becomes the family business. In 2012 he quit claims adjusting, and now devotes all his time to our restaurants.

I knew Phil had a great palate and appetite for excellent food, but I didn't realize that he had another set of skills that are perfect for the restaurant business. His official titles are Waffle Hustler (at Brown Sugar Kitchen) and Rib Wrangler (at B-Side BBQ). He's really a jack-of-all-trades. You may find him working at the door during Sunday brunch while I'm cooking in the kitchen. Most evenings, he heads over to B-Side BBQ, where he watches over things from his perch behind the bar while he mixes cocktails. If I had to give Phil one more title, it would be "vibe-ologist," as he's always making sure the music, the lighting, and the vibe are just right. He'll tell you that his favorite thing to do is to put together playlists that keep us dancing on the line. My favorite is one he calls the Waffle Mix. It was the first playlist he made back in 2008 shortly after Brown Sugar Kitchen opened, and though I've listened to it hundreds of times, it never gets old.

Gene Harris & the Three Sounds: Sitting Duck

Quincy Jones: Summer in the City

Sly & Robbie: Yes We Can

Connie Price & the Keystones: Sucker Punch

Dennis Bovell: Smouche

Nicole Willis & the Soul Investigators: Feeling Free

The Heptones: Book of Rules

Tony! Toni! Toné!: Thinking of You

Dianne Reeves: Down Here on the Ground

Nat "King" Cole: Calypso Blues (one of my favorites!)

Darondo: Didn't I

Asa: Fire on the Mountain

Betty Wright: Clean Up Woman

Sugarhill Gang: Rapper's Reprise

Lightning Head: N.P.G.

Shirley Bassey: Light My Fire

Estelle: Wait a Minute (Just a Touch)

Al Green: Lay It Down

CHAPTER 3
VEGETABLES
& SIDES

I grew up eating vegetables cooked Southern style, which, more often than not, meant they were cooked for hours and seasoned with pork. Then I went to France and discovered vegetables prepared with a bit of bite left in them and seasoned with things like fresh herbs and olive oil. It was a revelation. At Brown Sugar Kitchen, I take the vegetables I grew up eating—black-eyed peas, sweet potatoes, and collard greens—and prepare them using techniques I learned abroad. These days I sauté my collard greens in olive oil and season them with red onion and garlic instead of fatback, and roast green beans instead of boiling them. Writing for Citysearch, Bryan Miller, a former *New York Times* restaurant critic, said that I cook like your grandmother, if your "grandmother has a diploma from a Paris cooking school." I like to think he was talking about my vegetables.

People are often surprised to learn that we don't add pork to our collards, but I made a conscious decision when I opened the restaurant to keep the side dishes meat-free. It's important to me that that our vegetarian customers feel as welcome as the omnivores.

Side dishes play a large role on a Southern-influenced menu, and Southern cooks have historically been known as much for their signature side dishes as their main courses. We honor this tradition by highlighting them on our menus as well.

ROASTED GREEN BEANS WITH SESAME-SEED DRESSING

I can get a little bored with green beans. I really enjoy them mixed with other vegetables in salads, but alone I think they need some finesse. Sesame seeds made their way into the Southern kitchen with the slaves who were brought here from Africa. Often called *benne* seeds in the South, they were one of the many exotic ingredients brought to this country that we now take for granted. Photographer Jody Horton and his team thought these made excellent finger food.

Preheat the oven to 450°F/230°C and set a rack to the top position. Line a rimmed baking sheet with parchment paper.

In a small bowl, stir together the garlic, oil, vinegar, tahini, sesame seeds, and red pepper flakes. Add the green beans and toss until evenly coated. Season with salt and black pepper.

Spread the beans in a single layer on the prepared baking sheet and roast, tossing occasionally, until tender and lightly browned, about 20 minutes. Serve immediately.

3 garlic cloves, smashed

½ CUP/120 ML extra-virgin olive oil

2 TBSP Champagne vinegar

2 TBSP tahini

1 TBSP sesame seeds

1 TSP red pepper flakes

1 LB/455 G green beans, trimmed

Coarse salt and freshly ground black pepper

SIMPLY SAUTÉED
COLLARD GREENS

True to my Southern heritage, I grew up eating collard greens that were cooked for a long time. As I learned when I visited a plantation in Georgia, part of this tradition began when slaves left pots of food cooking while they tended the fields. Since tough cuts of meat were used to season the greens, the long cooking was necessary to tenderize the meat. At Brown Sugar Kitchen, we've left that tradition behind. I've found that sautéing the greens briefly in olive oil and seasoning them with garlic and red pepper flakes makes a great-tasting dish.

4 LB/1.8 KG collard greens, large stems removed

2 TBSP olive oil

1 red onion, sliced

4 garlic cloves, minced

1 TSP red pepper flakes

Kosher salt and freshly ground black pepper

Stack 5 to 7 collard greens, roll them like a cigar, and slice into thin strips. Repeat with the remaining collard greens.

In a large sauté pan, heat the oil over medium heat until shimmering. Add the onion, garlic, and red pepper flakes, and cook, stirring occasionally, until the onion and garlic are softened but not brown, about 3 minutes.

Add the sliced collards to the pan. Using tongs, toss the collards with the oil and onions, cooking just until the collards are bright green, about 2 minutes. Season with salt and black pepper. Serve immediately.

(To make ahead, refrigerate in an airtight container for up to 3 days. Reheat in a small saucepan with a small amount of water over medium heat.)

SUMMER SQUASH
SUCCOTASH

All that many people know of this dish is Sylvester the cat famously stuttering "sufferin' suc-cotash," on the Saturday-morning cartoons. But succotash is an actual dish, and a very good one too. The name comes from a Native American term that describes boiled vegetables. There are several regional variations, but most contain corn, lima beans, or both, cooked in a buttery broth. Here I've added summer squash and included black-eyed peas instead of limas. I think this combination of vegetables and beans really flatter one another, with con-trasting colors, textures, and flavors.

In a large bowl, cover the black-eyed peas with 2 to 3 in/5 to 7.5 cm of cold water and let soak overnight.

Drain and rinse the beans, and transfer them to a large soup pot. Add enough fresh cold water to cover the beans by about 3 in/ 7.5 cm. Bring to a boil, reduce to a simmer, and cook until peas are tender, 30 to 40 minutes. Drain the peas and let cool to room temperature.

In a large saucepan, melt the butter over medium heat. Add the green onions, bell pepper, garlic, squash, corn, and ½ tsp salt and cook until the vegetables are tender, about 15 minutes.

Stir in the black-eyed peas and the stock and bring to a simmer. Add the sour cream, nutmeg, cayenne, and thyme. Reduce the heat to medium-low and simmer until the mixture is slightly thickened, about 8 minutes. Season with salt and black pepper. Serve immediately.

¾ CUP/150 G dried black-eyed peas

1 TBSP unsalted butter

6 green onions, white and green parts, chopped

½ red bell pepper, chopped

1 garlic clove, minced

1 LB/455 G summer squash, such as zucchini and yellow crookneck, diced

2 CUPS/490 G fresh corn kernels (from about 2 ears)

Kosher salt

1 CUP/240 ML chicken stock

⅓ CUP/75 ML sour cream or crème fraîche

¼ TSP grated nutmeg

¼ TSP cayenne pepper

1 TSP chopped fresh thyme

Freshly ground black pepper

OKRA
PEPERONATA

For this updated dish of stewed okra and tomatoes, I look to Southern Italy for bell peppers and onion along with some fresh herbs and balsamic vinegar. This mixture makes a great vegetarian main course served with grits cakes (see page 47) or an accompaniment to smoked meats. When shopping, look for small okra pods. They're ideal for this dish.

1 LB/455 G okra, trimmed

3 TBSP olive oil

1 large red onion, halved and sliced

Kosher salt

2 red bell peppers, seeded and sliced into ¼-in/6-mm strips

2 yellow or orange bell peppers, seeded and sliced into ¼-in/ 6-mm strips

1¼ LB/570 G tomatoes, seeded and chopped

2 garlic cloves, minced

1 TSP fresh thyme

1 TSP fresh oregano

1 TSP sweet paprika

¼ TSP cayenne pepper

⅓ CUP/75 ML water

1 TBSP finely chopped fresh basil leaves

2 TBSP balsamic vinegar

Freshly ground black pepper

If the okra pods are small, leave them whole; otherwise cut into 1-in/2.5-cm pieces.

In a wide sauté pan, heat 2 tbsp of the oil over medium-high heat until shimmering. Add the onion and a pinch of salt and cook, stirring occasionally, until the onions start to brown, about 8 minutes. Add the remaining 1 tbsp oil, the okra, red and yellow bell peppers, and a pinch of salt and cook, stirring occasionally, until the peppers soften and the vegetables start to brown, 10 to 15 minutes.

Add the tomatoes, garlic, thyme, oregano, paprika, cayenne, and water. Cover partially and bring to a simmer. Reduce the heat to medium and cook, stirring occasionally, until the vegetables are tender, about 10 minutes. Uncover the pan, stir in the basil and vinegar, and cook for about 30 seconds more. Season with salt and pepper. Serve immediately.

GREEN CHILE–HARISSA POTATO GRATIN

There was a point in my career when I became obsessed with North African flavors. It began while I was living in France when I made an Algerian friend who made couscous from scratch. Later I discovered Paula Wolfert's wonderful book *Couscous and Other Good Food from Morocco.* And then I went to work at a restaurant where *ras el hanout* and harissa were incorporated into French bistro-style dishes. Traditionally, harissa—an aromatic spice paste—is made with a red *piri piri* chile, but here I've made a green chile harissa to give a kick to a classic potato gratin.

GREEN HARISSA
1 poblano chile
1 small jalapeño chile
¼ CUP/60 ML olive oil
1 small yellow onion, chopped
2 garlic cloves, chopped
1 TSP fresh thyme
PINCH of turmeric
PINCH of ground cinnamon
PINCH of ground cloves
1½ TSP honey
2 TBSP chopped fresh mint

2½ LB/1.2 KG russet potatoes, peeled and cut into thin slices
Kosher salt and freshly ground pepper
1 CUP/240 ML heavy cream

Preheat the oven to 400°F/200°C.

To make the harissa: Rub the poblano and jalapeño with 1 tsp of the oil and wrap loosely in aluminum foil. Roast until very tender, about 1 hour. Let the poblano and jalapeño cool in the foil. Peel off the skins and remove the cores, seeds, and stems.

Meanwhile, in a small sauté pan, heat 1 tbsp oil over medium heat until shimmering. Add the onion and garlic, and cook until the onion is tender and translucent, about 10 minutes. Stir in the thyme, turmeric, cinnamon, and cloves and let cool.

In a blender or food processor, combine the onion mixture, the poblano, jalapeño, honey, mint, and the remaining 8 tsp/40 ml olive oil and process to a coarse paste.

Reduce the oven temperature to 350°F/180°C. In a 1½-qt/1.4-L baking dish, spread about a quarter of the potato slices in a single layer. Season lightly with salt and pepper and spread about 2 tbsp of the harissa paste on top and cover with about ¼ cup/60 ml of the cream. Repeat three more times, until all the potatoes, harissa, and cream have been used, ending with a layer of harissa.

Bake until the potatoes are tender when pierced with a knife, about 1 hour. If the top begins to brown too much, cover with a sheet of aluminum foil. Let cool for about 15 minutes. Serve warm.

(To make ahead, refrigerate the cooked potato gratin for up to 3 days. Reheat in a 350°F/180°C oven until heated through, about 25 minutes.)

BAKED SWEET POTATO WEDGES

I spent months trying to make sweet potato fries, before I realized that I just didn't feel that immersing them in oil enhanced the texture or flavor. I wanted to make something simpler and more healthful but still delicious, and this is it. I like these with a side of buttermilk dressing. It makes a cool, creamy contrast to balance the spicy flavors of the sweet potatoes.

Preheat the oven to 350°F/180°C. Line a baking sheet with parchment paper.

Prick each sweet potato several times with a fork and put on the prepared baking sheet. Bake until tender when pierced with a fork, about 30 minutes. Remove from the oven and let cool slightly.

Cut each sweet potato lengthwise into 1-in /2.5-cm wedges.

Arrange wedges on one layer on the baking sheet and season with salt, the olive oil, and the Creole Spice Mix. Bake an additional 5 minutes, then flip the wedges and bake another 5 to 7 minutes, until crisp and slightly browned.

Arrange the wedges on a serving platter and serve immediately.

3 LB/1.4 KG red-skinned sweet potatoes, scrubbed and unpeeled

Kosher salt

2 TBSP olive oil, plus more if needed

2 TSP Creole Spice Mix [page 51]

SMOKED MASHED
SWEET POTATOES

We fuel our smoker with applewood and oak, a combination we find subtler than the hickory we use at B-Side, our barbecue joint. It's perfect for these sweet potatoes. We discovered through trial and error that 13 minutes is just the right amount of time to give the potatoes a gentle smoky taste that doesn't mask their natural sweetness. You'll be amazed at how easy the smoking process is and how much flavor it adds to this simple dish.

2 LB/910 G orange-fleshed sweet potatoes, peeled and quartered

6 TBSP/90 ML pure maple syrup

¼ CUP/60 ML heavy cream

4 TBSP/55 G unsalted butter, melted, plus THIN SLICE of unsalted butter, at room temperature

PINCH of cayenne pepper

Kosher salt

Preheat the oven to 425°F/220°C.

In an ovenproof baking dish, spread the sweet potatoes in a single layer. Add just enough water to come ¼ in/6 mm up the sides of the potatoes and cover with aluminum foil. Bake until the potatoes are almost tender, about 45 minutes.

Ignite an electric grill and set to 200°F/95°C, or start a small fire in a charcoal grill. If using an electric grill, place hickory, mesquite, or any other aromatic wood chips in a piece of foil and punch holes in the foil with a fork. Set the foil package on top of the grill grates. (If using a charcoal grill, place the wood chips directly on the charcoal.)

Set the baking dish with the sweet potatoes on the grate. Cover the grill and allow the sweet potatoes to smoke for 13 minutes.

If using a food processor, combine the sweet potatoes, maple syrup, cream, melted butter, and cayenne and process until smooth. (If mixing by hand, in a large bowl, mash until smooth.) If the sweet potatoes are too thick, stir in a little water. Taste and season with salt.

Transfer to a serving bowl and top with the room-temperature butter. Serve immediately.

BBQ BAKED BEANS

This is the only side dish at B-Side BBQ that isn't vegetarian. To make up for that, I've included almost every part of the pig here except for the oink. I've made a meatless version, but frankly it's not the same. Of course, you can omit anything you don't care for and it will still taste great. This is one of several sides that could work as a meal. Slow cooking is the key to deep flavor.

In a large bowl, cover the navy beans with 2 to 3 in/5 to 7.5 cm of cold water and let soak overnight.

Drain and rinse the beans, and transfer them to a large soup pot. Add the onion quarters, garlic, and ham hock and enough fresh cold water to cover the beans by about 1 in/2.5 cm. Bring to a boil, reduce to a simmer, and cook until the beans are tender, about 1 hour. Drain the beans, reserving the cooking liquid, and transfer them to an ovenproof baking dish. Pull the meat off the ham hock and reserve, discarding the bone. Discard the onion quarters and garlic.

Preheat the oven to 350°F/180°C. In a medium saucepan, cook the bacon and diced onion until the bacon fat is rendered and the onion is translucent, about 5 minutes. Add the tomatoes and their juice, ketchup, molasses, Worcestershire sauce, Tabasco sauce, brown sugar, salt, black pepper, cayenne, and dry mustard. Bring to a boil, reduce to a simmer, and cook until flavors are combined, about 5 minutes.

Add the sauce, reserved ham, and cooked pork, if using, to the beans and stir gently to combine. Moisten with some of the reserved bean cooking liquid and cover with aluminum foil. Bake, stirring occasionally, until the beans are soft but not falling apart, about 2 hours. Add additional bean cooking liquid, if needed, to keep the beans moist. Let stand for 10 minutes to thicken. Serve immediately.

(To make ahead, refrigerate in an airtight container for up to 3 days. Reheat in a small saucepan over medium heat.)

2¼ CUPS/455 G dried navy beans, picked over and rinsed

1 large yellow onion, half quartered, half diced

2 garlic cloves, peeled

1 small smoked ham hock

8 OZ/225 G bacon, diced

ONE 14.5-oz/415-g can diced tomatoes

½ CUP/120 G ketchup

3 TBSP molasses

1 TBSP Worcestershire sauce

1 TSP Tabasco sauce

¼ CUP/50 G firmly packed brown sugar

1 TSP kosher salt

¼ TSP freshly ground black pepper

¼ TSP cayenne pepper

¼ TSP dry mustard

½ CUP/90 G diced cooked pork (optional)

DIRTY RICE

I know what you're thinking . . . why would anyone want to eat something "dirty?" This dish originally earned the "dirty" moniker from the crisp bits of chicken gizzards and giblets scattered through the rice. We offer a vegetarian version at Brown Sugar Kitchen, but this original recipe with all the fixings is my favorite. A bit like a rice stuffing, it's spicy and filling enough for a meal, but also makes a great side dish for roast chicken or pork.

1½ CUPS/310 G basmati rice

2 TBSP vegetable oil

8 OZ/225 G chicken livers, trimmed

1 LB/445 G bulk pork sausage

1 white onion, finely chopped

1 green bell pepper, diced

1 red bell pepper, diced

1 TBSP minced garlic

1 TBSP chopped jalapeño chile

¼ CUP/60 ML Worcestershire sauce

2 bay leaves

1 TBSP chopped fresh thyme

2 TSP freshly ground black pepper

1 TSP kosher salt

½ TSP sweet paprika

PINCH of cayenne pepper

4 green onions, white and green parts, chopped

In a large bowl, cover the rice with 2 to 3 in/5 to 7.5 cm of cold water. Stir the rice with your hand and drain. Repeat five or six times, until the water runs clear.

Transfer the washed rice to a medium heavy-bottomed pot. Add enough fresh cold water to cover the rice by about 1 in/2.5 cm. Bring to a boil, reduce to a simmer, cover, and cook until the rice is tender, about 20 minutes. Do not overcook.

In a large sauté pan, heat the oil over medium-high heat until shimmering. Add the livers and sausage and cook, stirring occasionally and breaking up the sausage with the back of the spoon, until the meat is no longer pink, 7 to 8 minutes. With a slotted spoon, transfer the livers and sausage to a small bowl. Add the onion, green and red bell peppers, garlic, and jalapeño to the pan, and cook over medium-high heat until the vegetables are soft, stirring occasionally, about 10 minutes.

Meanwhile, chop the chicken livers into small dice. Return them to the sauté pan, along with the sausage, Worcestershire sauce, and the cooked rice. Stir until the rice is fully incorporated. Stir in the bay leaves, thyme, black pepper, salt, paprika, cayenne, and green onions. Partially cover the pan, reduce the heat to low, and cook until the flavors are well blended, about 15 minutes. Remove bay leaves, discard, and serve immediately.

MACARONI & CHEESE

Like politics and religion, macaroni and cheese is a topic sure to polarize any family gathering. To bake or not to bake? One cheese or three? Bread crumbs or none? The list goes on. Obviously, I created this version to my taste, but as it's one of the most popular sides I make, I think I've hit upon an exceptional version. I must thank my college roommates who ate macaroni and cheese out of a box when we met. They inspired me to help them do better. Abs and El, this one's for you!

Preheat the oven to 350°F/180°C. Butter a 2-qt/2-L baking dish.

In a large pot of boiling salted water, cook the macaroni until tender, 10 to 12 minutes. Drain.

In a large heavy-bottomed saucepan, melt 2 tbsp of the butter over medium heat. Stir in the flour, salt, Worcestershire sauce, garlic, and ginger until blended. Cook for 1 minute, without browning. Gradually pour in the cream and milk and whisk until combined. Cook, whisking constantly, until the sauce thickens slightly, about 10 minutes.

Remove saucepan from heat and stir in the Cheddar until melted. Stir in the white pepper and Tabasco sauce. Add the cooked macaroni and toss to coat. Transfer to the prepared baking dish.

In a small frying pan, melt the remaining 3 tbsp butter over medium heat. Add the bread crumbs and toss to coat. Sprinkle the bread crumbs over the macaroni. Bake until the sauce is bubbly and the crumbs are browned, about 25 minutes. Let rest for 10 minutes before serving.

8 OZ/225 G elbow macaroni

5 TBSP/70 G unsalted butter, plus more for the pan

2 TBSP all-purpose flour

½ TSP kosher salt

½ TSP Worcestershire sauce

½ TSP chopped garlic

⅛ TSP grated fresh ginger

¾ CUP/180 ML heavy cream

¾ CUP/180 ML whole milk

8 OZ/225 G sharp Cheddar cheese, grated

PINCH of ground white pepper

DASH of Tabasco sauce

1 CUP/55 G fresh bread crumbs

HERBED MUSHROOM SPOON BREAD

Spoon bread is a lovely hybrid of a dish, claiming the middle ground between cornbread and soufflé. It's also wonderfully versatile in that it can be eaten at breakfast, lunch, or dinner, either as a side dish or a main course. This is a great recipe for adventurous cooks. Try it with different varieties of mushrooms—cremlnis, portobellos, or even truffles if you're feeling flush. Each brings its distinct flavor to the dish.

Preheat the oven to 350°F/180°C. Butter a 1½-qt/1.4-L baking or soufflé dish.

In a sauté pan, melt 2 tbsp of the butter over medium heat. Add the shallots and cook until softened, stirring occasionally, about 3 minutes. Add the mushrooms and thyme, season with salt and pepper, and cook, stirring occasionally, until the mushrooms are cooked and any liquid has evaporated, about 8 minutes. Remove from the heat.

In a heavy-bottomed saucepan, heat the milk over medium-high heat until bubbles form around the edges. Slowly whisk in the cornmeal, reduce the heat to low, and cook, whisking constantly, until the mixture thickens, about 10 minutes. Remove from the heat and stir in the remaining 2 tbsp butter and the Cheddar cheese. Add the egg yolks, one at a time, whisking to combine after each addition.

In a medium bowl, whip the egg whites until medium-stiff peaks form—the tips of the peaks curl down slightly when the beaters are lifted. Gently fold the whipped egg whites into the batter. Pour the mixture into the prepared baking dish.

Bake until the spoon bread is puffed and golden brown, about 50 minutes. Serve immediately.

4 TBSP/55 G unsalted butter, plus more for the pan

3 shallots, minced

1 LB/455 G button mushrooms, sliced

1 TSP fresh thyme

Kosher salt and freshly ground pepper

3 CUPS/720 ML whole milk

1 CUP/140 G cornmeal

2 OZ/55 G Cheddar cheese, grated

4 eggs, separated

BUTTERMILK
CORNBREAD

I grew up eating Jiffy cornbread, a boxed mix that required the addition of milk or water. I'm pretty sure my mother doctored it up with some melted butter too. Convenience was key for her and I can appreciate that. But at Brown Sugar Kitchen we don't take shortcuts. My cornbread has customers swooning. I think it's the balance of sweet and salty that makes it so popular. It's also not quite cakey and not quite dense—its texture is just right. Try making this once, and hopefully this will be the last cornbread recipe you will ever need. Cornbread is best eaten fresh. Use any leftovers to make croutons (see page 116) or Buttermilk Cornbread Pudding (page 168).

1 egg

1½ CUPS/360 ML buttermilk

1 CUP/125 G all-purpose flour

1 CUP/140 G cornmeal

4 TSP baking powder

½ TSP baking soda

2 TSP kosher salt

1 TBSP sugar

½ CUP/115 G unsalted butter, melted, plus 1 TBSP for the pan

¾ CUP/185 G cooked fresh corn kernels (optional)

Preheat the oven to 425°F/220°C. Put a 12-in/30.5-cm cast-iron skillet in the oven to preheat.

In a large bowl, whisk together the egg and buttermilk. In a medium bowl, mix together the flour, cornmeal, baking powder, baking soda, salt, and sugar. Add the flour mixture to the buttermilk mixture and mix with a wooden spoon; do not overmix. Stir in the melted butter. If using, gently fold the corn kernels into the batter until just combined.

Remove the skillet from the oven and add the 1 tbsp butter to the hot skillet. When the butter melts, brush it evenly over the bottom and sides of the skillet. Pour the batter into the skillet.

Bake until the cornbread is browned on the edges and a toothpick stuck in the center comes out clean, 20 to 25 minutes. Let cool slightly. Serve warm.

MILDRED HOWARD

ARTIST AND COOK

*Her artwork has been displayed at the De Young Museum,
the San Francisco Museum of Modern Art, and shown
internationally in Berlin, Cairo, and at the Venice Biennial*

Lives: Berkeley, since 1948

Regular order: Granola

I first discovered Tanya when I would watch her cooking
show, *Melting Pot* "Soul Kitchen," on the Food Network.
I would think to myself, "She knows how to cook." That's
what impressed me initially. And then I went to a party that
she catered. The party was over and I looked in the kitchen
and there she was. The next thing I know, she's here in sweet
West Oakland. I think it's so fabulous for her to come into this
community and make Southern cooking in a relatively healthy
way. That's what I like about it. She uses really good ingredients. I like her presence too. Whenever you see the owner of a
restaurant cooking you know things are right.

CHAPTER 4
SOUPS & SANDWICHES

An outstanding sandwich makes me think of a (don't laugh) gospel choir. When every-one is singing their part, the magic occurs all around them. An oyster po'boy needs a roll that's both soft and crusty, but you don't want the oysters to get lost in the bread, so the roll can't be too doughy. A dose of spicy coleslaw brings a needed bit of acid to the party, and an even schmear of aïoli brings all the flavors into line while letting the oys-ters shine. It takes a practiced hand and an experienced palate to make these things happen. But when it works, there's nothing better than a perfectly composed sandwich that's just the right amount of filling, bread, and condiments.

In this chapter there are also a few dishes that I would consider for a first course at a dinner party, like my riff on traditional French onion soup, where I use sweet Vidalia onions from Georgia and cornbread croutons rather than the country-style loaf called for in most recipes. I even take a Spanish gazpacho and give it a Creole flavor. Some of the dishes here can make a meal, like my chili made from burnt ends of barbecued brisket. It's also ideal potluck fare. Easy to transport and reheat, and everyone loves it.

CREOLE GAZPACHO

Chilled gazpacho is a terrific way to enjoy an excess of summer tomatoes. Make a batch after a weekend trip to the farmers' market and you're set for a week's worth of quick lunches. But you don't have to save this for tomato season—you can substitute canned tomatoes and make it all year-round.

In a food processor, pulse together the tomatoes and their juices, the bell pepper, onion, cucumber, cilantro, parsley, olive oil, lemon juice, vinegar, ½ tsp salt, and the Creole Spice Mix until smooth. Transfer the gazpacho to a nonreactive container and refrigerate for at least for 4 hours or up to overnight.

Just before serving, season with salt, pepper, and hot pepper sauce. Serve cold, garnished with parsley.

(To make ahead, refrigerate in an airtight container for up to 3 days.)

1 LB/455 G tomatoes, peeled, seeded, and diced, or ONE 14½-oz/415-g can diced tomatoes

1 red bell pepper, seeded and diced

½ yellow onion, diced

1 cucumber, peeled, seeded, and diced

1 TBSP chopped fresh cilantro

1 TBSP chopped fresh parsley

1 TBSP olive oil

Juice of 1 lemon

1½ TSP red wine vinegar

Kosher salt

1½ TSP Creole Spice Mix (page 51)

Freshly ground pepper

Hot pepper sauce

Parsley or chervil for garnish

SPICED WINTER SQUASH SOUP

Since you can't really buy half a squash, I'm suggesting you make a large pot of this soup and freeze whatever you can't eat right away. Although, you might not find that necessary once you taste this soup, which is the ultimate comfort food. Just add a thick slice of toasted bread and a simple green salad, and dinner is ready.

1 large yellow onion, cut into chunks

2 tart apples, such as Granny Smith, cored, peeled, and quartered

2 TBSP plus ½ TSP olive oil

1 butternut squash, halved and seeded

1 acorn squash, halved and seeded

1 delicata squash, halved and seeded

2 TBSP unsalted butter, cut into cubes, at room temperature

6 sprigs thyme

1 head garlic

1 TBSP grated fresh ginger

1 TSP sweet paprika

½ TSP ground cinnamon

¼ TSP cayenne pepper

1 TSP kosher salt

5 CUPS/1.2 L vegetable or chicken stock, plus more as needed

½ CUP/120 ML heavy cream

Freshly ground black pepper

Preheat the oven to 425°F/220°C. Line a rimmed baking sheet with parchment paper.

Spread the onion and apples on one side of the baking sheet and drizzle with 1 tbsp of the olive oil. Place the squash halves on the other side of the baking sheet, cut-side up. Dot the squash with the butter. Scatter the thyme sprigs over the vegetables.

Slice the top third off the head of garlic. Drizzle the garlic with ½ tsp olive oil, wrap it in aluminum foil, and put it on the baking sheet with the squash. Roast, stirring the onion and apples every 15 minutes, until everything is very tender, 1 hour to 1 hour 15 minutes. If any of the ingredients become tender before the others, transfer them to a bowl and set aside until the remaining ingredients are finished roasting. Let cool for about 15 minutes. Discard the thyme sprigs.

In a large soup pot, heat the remaining 1 tbsp olive oil over medium heat until shimmering. Add the ginger, paprika, cinnamon, and cayenne, and stir until they release their aromas, about 30 seconds. Remove from the heat.

Add the onion and apples to the pot. Scoop out the flesh of the squashes, and add to the pot, discarding the skins. Carefully squeeze the roasted garlic into the pot, discarding the papery skins. Add the salt and the stock. Bring to a simmer over medium heat, scraping any browned bits off the bottom of the pot. Simmer, stirring occasionally, for 15 minutes.

Remove the soup from the heat and let cool. In a food processor or using an immersion blender, purée the soup until smooth. Stir in the cream and season with salt and black pepper. Add more stock if needed to thin the soup to the desired consistency. Over low heat, gently warm the soup, stirring occasionally. Serve immediately.

(To make ahead, refrigerate in an airtight container for up to 3 days. Reheat in a soup pot over medium heat. Freeze for up to 1 month.)

VIDALIA ONION SOUP WITH CORNBREAD CROUTONS

A crunchy lid of cornbread croutons, a dash of hot sauce, and a base of sweet onions give this bistro classic a Southern soul. Vidalia onions are named for the region in Georgia where they originated, and they can be found in markets from late April through August. If they're not available, look for another variety of sweet onion such as Maui or Walla Walla. The cornbread croutons add a wonderful flavor to the soup and can easily be made a day ahead.

2 TBSP unsalted butter

2 LB/910 G Vidalia or other sweet onions, halved and thinly sliced

¼ CUP/60 ML dry sherry

6 CUPS/1.4 L chicken stock

3 garlic cloves

2 TSP chopped fresh thyme

2 TSP Tabasco or other hot pepper sauce

1 TSP kosher salt

¼ TSP freshly ground pepper

3¼ OZ/90 G Gruyère cheese, grated

CORNBREAD CROUTONS

3 OZ/85 G Buttermilk Cornbread (page 106), cut into 1-in/2.5-cm cubes

Olive oil for drizzling

Kosher salt

In a large pot, melt the butter over medium-high heat. Add the onions and cook, stirring occasionally, until soft and browned, about 20 minutes.

Add the sherry and stir until most of the liquid has evaporated. Add the stock, garlic, and thyme. Bring to a boil, then add the hot pepper sauce, salt, and pepper. Reduce to a simmer and cook for about 10 minutes.

To make the croutons: Preheat the oven to 350°F/180°C. On a baking sheet, spread the cornbread in a single layer and drizzle with oil and sprinkle with salt. Bake, turning the croutons over once or twice, until they are lightly browned, about 15 minutes.

Turn off the oven, and preheat the broiler. Transfer the soup to six ovenproof crocks. Divide the croutons evenly among the crocks and sprinkle each crock with Gruyère. Place the crocks under the broiler until the Gruyère is bubbly and brown, about 2 minutes. Serve immediately.

BURNT ENDS CHILI

A meat lover's chili to be sure, this was inspired by the scraps from our smoked meats. When serving ribs in the restaurant, we cut from the center and serve the customers the meatiest and prettiest ones, but there are always some drier ends that we scrape off the bone and reserve for this chili. The same is true for our sliced brisket; we serve the customer the moist center cuts and chop the end pieces to stew in the moist chili broth. Choosing a variety of leftover smoked or grilled meats, or even some cooked ground beef, will help make this chili recipe your own.

In a large heavy-bottomed soup pot, heat the oil over medium heat until shimmering. Add the onion, bell pepper, jalapeño, and garlic and cook until the onion is tender and translucent, about 4 minutes. Add the ancho and New Mexico chile powders, cumin, garlic powder, 2 tsp salt, 1 tsp black pepper, cayenne, and bay leaf and cook, stirring occasionally, until the spices are warm and fragrant, about 2 minutes.

Add the stout, tomatoes and their juice, pinto beans, pork, ketchup, vinegar, Tabasco sauce, and stock. Bring to a boil, reduce to a simmer, and cook, stirring occasionally, for about 90 minutes, until the flavors meld. Season with salt and pepper. Serve immediately.

(To make ahead, refrigerate in an airtight container for up to 1 week. Reheat in a soup pot over medium heat.)

2 TBSP olive oil

1 large yellow onion, diced

1 red bell pepper, seeded and diced

1 TBSP minced jalapeño chile

4 garlic cloves, minced

1 TBSP ancho chile powder

1 TBSP New Mexico chile powder

2 TSP ground cumin

2 TSP garlic powder

Kosher salt and freshly ground black pepper

½ TSP cayenne pepper

1 bay leaf

¾ CUP/180 ML stout

ONE 15-oz/430-g can crushed tomatoes

TWO 15-oz/430-g cans pinto beans, drained and rinsed

2 CUPS/360 G diced cooked pork or beef, or 1 LB/455 G ground beef, cooked and drained

¾ CUP/220 G ketchup

⅓ CUP/75 ML apple cider vinegar

½ TSP Tabasco sauce

2½ CUPS/600 ML beef or chicken stock

ERA AND DON FARNSWORTH

MAGNOLIA EDITIONS, FINE ART PRINTERS

Works: West Oakland, since 1981

Regular order: Gumbo

This is an amazingly creative area, full of artists and crafts-people. There's a blacksmith across the street from us. Dorothy Lenahan's glass studio is here. Paul Discoe's Japanese joinery shop is here. There's even a samurai sword maker down the street. We were here when the earthquake happened in 1989. We ran out of the building and saw plumes of black smoke rising. Cars were burning. And then we thought, "The view looks different." It took a moment to register that the freeway was gone. We drove over to see if we could help take people to the hospital. Our neighbors brought ladders and forklifts to help pull people out of the rubble.

Southern culture is part of the heritage of this neighborhood. The people who live here are very friendly. Strangers say hello to each other on the street. People who aren't from West Oakland think it's strange. Brown Sugar Kitchen is part of that culture, not just for its food, but also in the art and the environment that has sprung up around it. It's a gem for this neighborhood. If you want a vibrant community you need diversity, not just in the people, but in the crafts and the businesses as well. A focal point like Brown Sugar Kitchen is important to get people excited about the neighborhood.

STEPHEN RADEMAKER

GENERAL CONTRACTOR, HANDYMAN FOR BROWN SUGAR KITCHEN, STAFF MEMBER AT KINETIC STEAM WORKS

Lives: West Oakland, since 1994

Regular order: Grits and eggs

Our shop is throw-a-rock, break-a-window close to Brown Sugar Kitchen. I started working for Tanya and Phil when a friend asked if I could help fix their smoker. We're a good match—I like to eat and they like to cook and be great hosts. And they're very understanding of my needs as an oddball. When Brown Sugar Kitchen opened, it didn't take long for there to be a line around the corner. There's a longing for good food here, and Brown Sugar Kitchen helps fill that need. The restaurant was a precursor to the Oakland food revolution. It's amazing how many restaurants have opened here in the past few years. Brown Sugar Kitchen sent a message to other restaurateurs that they could succeed here.

TRACY HOBBS

STAFF MEMBER AT KINETIC STEAM WORKS

Lives: West Oakland, since 1995

Regular order: Extra biscuits, please

Kinetic Steam Works is part of West Oakland's industrial arts community that restores vintage steam engines for use in art performances. We consider ourselves steam dorks, not steam punks. It's not a fashion show for us. We work with real steam. This is a real technology. We do real things.

VEGETARIAN
MUFFULETTA

The legendary muffuletta served at Central Grocery is one of my favorite reasons to visit New Orleans. The market is an institution, and the sandwich is always consistent—my ultimate judgment of a great food establishment. The olive salad and layers of cured meats marry perfectly with the crusty Italian bread. It's just the thing to line the stomach before or after several Sazeracs. I developed this vegetarian version for a catering client and realized it was a keeper.

2 red bell peppers

OLIVE SALAD
3 TBSP Pickled Vegetables [page 129]
⅓ CUP/40 G pitted green olives
3 TBSP pitted black olives
1 TBSP roasted red bell pepper
1 TBSP pickled pepperoncini pepper
1½ TBSP capers, rinsed
1 garlic clove, peeled
2½ TSP extra-virgin olive oil
1¼ TSP chopped fresh parsley
1¼ TSP chopped fresh oregano
1¼ TSP chopped fresh basil
Kosher salt and freshly ground pepper

1 large eggplant
2 medium zucchini
1 TBSP olive oil
Kosher salt and freshly ground pepper
8 slices provolone cheese
4 soft white bread rolls, halved

Roast the bell peppers over a gas flame or under a broiler until blackened on all sides, turning occasionally. Place the peppers in a small bowl and cover tightly with plastic wrap. Set aside for 30 minutes, until the skin is loosened from the peppers. Peel off the skin and trim the peppers, removing the core, seeds, and stems. Cut the peppers lengthwise into strips and reserve several strips for the dressing.

To make the olive salad: Roughly chop the pickled vegetables, green and black olives, roasted red pepper, pepperoncini pepper, capers, and garlic. (You can do this step in a food processor, but just give it a couple of pulses. It should be fairly coarse.)

In a medium bowl, combine the chopped vegetables, the olive oil, parsley, oregano, and basil. Season with salt and pepper. (To make ahead, refrigerate in an airtight container for up to 1 month.)

Preheat the oven to 500°F/260°C. Line a baking sheet with aluminum foil or parchment paper.

Trim the ends from the eggplant and zucchini and cut lengthwise into ½-in/12-mm slabs. Toss the eggplant and zucchini with the oil, and season with salt and pepper. Spread the eggplant and zucchini in a single layer on the prepared baking sheet. Roast for 10 minutes, until the undersides are lightly browned. Carefully turn over, and continue roasting until softened, about 10 minutes more.

Place 2 slices of provolone on the bottom of each roll. Top with bell pepper, eggplant, and zucchini. Place a heaping spoonful of olive salad on top of the roasted vegetables, and cover with the top of the roll. Serve immediately.

(To make ahead, cover tightly with plastic wrap and refrigerate overnight.)

BBQ PULLED-PORK SANDWICH

What do you expect of your pulled pork? Is it chopped? Is your sauce vinegar-based or tomato-based? Is your roll soft or crusty? Well, I love it all. For my restaurants, I couldn't decide and didn't really want the customers to have to decide. So we offer a variety at B-Side, but for Brown Sugar Kitchen, we always serve pulled pork with a traditional tomato-based sauce. It's a little spicy, a little sweet, and another favorite when you need a break from chicken and waffles.

Prepare a gas or charcoal grill for indirect cooking over medium heat. Lightly oil the grill grates. If using a charcoal grill, set a drip pan in the center of the bottom of the grill and arrange the hot coals around it. (If using a gas grill, preheat the grill with burners on high.) Season the pork with salt and pepper. Set the pork, fat-side up, on the grate. (If using a gas grill, turn off the burner directly under the grill, and reduce the other burners to medium heat.) Cover the grill and cook until the meat reaches an internal temperature of 150°F/65°C, 4 to 6 hours.

To make the sauce: In a medium saucepan, melt the butter over medium heat. Add the onion and garlic, and cook until the onion is tender and translucent, about 5 minutes. Add the vinegar, water, dry mustard, mustard seeds, cayenne, Worcestershire sauce, lemon juice, honey, red pepper flakes, turmeric, garlic powder, salt, and pepper. Bring to a boil, reduce to a simmer, and cook until thick and flavorful, about 45 minutes.

Preheat the oven to 350°F/180°C. Allow the cooked pork roast to rest for 15 minutes, then pull it apart with two forks, discarding bones, fat, and skin. Transfer pork to a large ovenproof baking dish. Add the sauce and toss until the pork is evenly coated. Cover with aluminum foil and bake until the shredded pork is hot, about 30 minutes.

Place the pork on the hamburger buns and top with 1/3 cup/40 g of coleslaw per sandwich. Serve immediately.

5 TO 7 LB/2.3 TO 3.2 KG bone-in pork shoulder roast
Kosher salt and freshly ground black pepper

BARBECUE SAUCE
1 TBSP unsalted butter
1 large white onion, chopped
6 garlic cloves, minced
¾ CUP/180 ML apple cider vinegar
¾ CUP/180 ML water
2 TSP dry mustard
1 TBSP yellow mustard seeds
¼ TSP cayenne pepper
1½ TSP Worcestershire sauce
Juice of 1 lemon
1½ TSP honey
1½ TSP red pepper flakes
¼ TSP turmeric
¼ TSP garlic powder
1 TSP kosher salt
½ TSP freshly ground black pepper

10 TO 12 French rolls or hamburger buns
1 RECIPE Spicy Green Coleslaw (page 82)

FRIED OYSTER PO'BOY

How do you fry oysters so that they're crisp on the outside yet still juicy? It all comes down to the temperature of the oil. Fry at too low a temperature, and your oysters will be soggy and greasy; too high and they will be burnt and dry. Invest in a deep-fry thermometer and make sure your oil is heated to 350°F/180°C. Use a high-quality neutral oil, such as canola or rice bran, and a heavy-bottomed pot. Don't be intimidated by frying. It can be safe and clean if you take your time and pay attention. There are many variations of hot and cold po'boys in New Orleans, but the common thread is the bread, usually a soft French roll. We use one from a local baker that's slightly wider than a hot dog bun. It's the perfect foil for the goodness that's inside.

Put the oysters in a small bowl and cover with the buttermilk.

In a large cast-iron frying pan, add oil to a depth of 1 in/2.5 cm. Heat the oil over medium heat until it reaches 350°F/180°C on an instant-read thermometer. The oil should be hot but not smoking. Line a rimmed baking sheet with paper towels and set a wire rack on top.

In a shallow dish, combine the cornmeal, flour, and Creole Spice Mix. Using a slotted spoon and letting any excess buttermilk drip back into the bowl, transfer the oysters to the cornmeal mixture. Toss the oysters in the cornmeal mixture until they are well coated.

Fry the oysters, a few at a time, taking care not to crowd the pan, turning once, until golden, about 3 minutes. Transfer to the rack over the baking sheet. Repeat with the remaining oysters.

Fill each roll with about ½ cup/60 g slaw, top with 5 hot oysters, and a dollop of mayonnaise, if desired. Serve immediately.

20 shucked oysters from a jar, drained and rinsed

1 CUP/240 ML buttermilk

Canola or rice bran oil for frying

1 CUP/140 G cornmeal

1 CUP/125 G all-purpose flour

2 TSP Creole Spice Mix (page 51)

4 soft French rolls, split, toasted, and buttered

2 CUPS/240 G Spicy Green Coleslaw (page 82)

Mayonnaise for dolloping (optional)

CARIBBEAN LOBSTER ROLL

For me, summer isn't complete without eating a lobster roll or two, a tradition that started during my first summer cooking job on Martha's Vineyard. It doesn't take much, just some lobster and a little homemade mayonnaise. Here, I bring a little island flavor to the New England classic with a spicy lime aïoli that includes a bit of curry spice and jalapeño chile. Pour a glass of champagne, and you've got a party! This is one of my favorite meals to enjoy with my hubby.

¼ CUP/50 G kosher salt

8 CUPS/2 L water

TWO 1¼-lb/570-g live lobsters

3 green onions, white and green parts, thinly sliced

3 TBSP Spicy Lime Aïoli (facing page)

4 good-quality hot dog buns, split

2 TBSP unsalted butter, at room temperature

In a large stockpot, combine the salt and water and bring to a boil over high heat. Add the lobsters, cover, and bring the water to a boil again. Reduce the heat to low and cook until shells are deep red, 10 to 12 minutes. Transfer the lobsters to a rimmed baking sheet and let cool. When cool enough to handle, crack the lobster shell and remove the meat from the claws and the tail.

In a medium bowl, combine the lobster meat and green onions. Stir in the lime aïoli.

Preheat the broiler and position an oven rack at least 6 in/15 cm below the broiler element. Spread the inside of the buns with the butter, place the buns on a baking sheet, and broil until golden brown, about 3 minutes. Fill each bun with one-quarter of the lobster mixture. Serve immediately.

SPICY LIME AÏOLI

In a blender or food processor, combine the egg yolk, garlic, lime juice, and lime zest and process until smooth. In a liquid measuring cup, combine the canola and olive oils. With the blender running, slowly drizzle in the oils until completely combined, about 2 minutes.

Scrape the aïoli into a small bowl. Stir in the jalapeño, curry powder, turmeric, cinnamon, cayenne, salt, black pepper, and cilantro. (To make ahead, refrigerate in an airtight container for up to 4 days.)

1 egg yolk

1 garlic clove, minced

1 TSP fresh lime juice

Zest from ½ lime

½ CUP/120 ML canola oil

2 TBSP extra-virgin olive oil

1 TSP minced jalapeño chile

1 TSP curry powder

¼ TSP turmeric

¼ TSP ground cinnamon

¼ TSP cayenne pepper

¼ TSP kosher salt

⅛ TSP freshly ground black pepper

1 TSP minced fresh cilantro

PICKLED SHRIMP
CRUDITÉ

There's an art to finding just the right appetizer. I'm always on the lookout for something with a sharpness that will spike an appetite, but it can't be too filling. I won't bother with a dish that's too fussy, and it's all the better if I can make it a day or two before a party. These briny, slightly spicy pickled shrimp win on all counts. I like to put them out with a platter of fresh radishes with salt and butter, crackers, and plenty of napkins.

1 LB/455 G medium shrimp

1 CUP/240 ML olive oil

⅓ CUP/75 ML fresh lemon juice, plus 1 lemon, unpeeled and thinly sliced

1 TSP coriander seeds

1 TSP celery seeds

1 TSP yellow mustard seeds

2 dried chiles de árbol

2 TSP peppercorns

2 bay leaves

2 garlic cloves, peeled

½ small red onion, thinly sliced

In a large pot of salted, boiling water, cook the shrimp until opaque, about 2 minutes. Drain and let cool. Peel the shrimp and remove the dark vein that runs down the back.

In a large bowl, combine the oil, lemon juice, coriander seeds, celery seeds, mustard seeds, chiles, peppercorns, bay leaves, garlic, lemon slices, and onion and toss until combined. Transfer to a large lidded glass jar or other nonreactive container, cover, and refrigerate at least 6 hours or up to 1 week.

Bring to room temperature, drain, and arrange on a serving platter. Serve with toothpicks.

PICKLED
VEGETABLES

Pickles don't have to be a big project. It takes just a few minutes to make the brine and assemble the vegetables for this quick recipe; there's no canning required. Simply put them in a jar in the refrigerator and they'll keep for up to a month. They're an essential part of my Vegetarian Muffuletta (page 120), and in fact, they go with just about any sandwich. Sometimes I'll put a few in a bowl to serve with cocktails and a plate of sliced salami.

Layer the cauliflower, carrots, radishes, onion, and jalapeños in a clean 1-qt/960-ml glass jar with a tight-fitting lid. (You can substitute several smaller jars or a glass bowl.)

In a large saucepan, combine the vinegar, water, coriander seeds, peppercorns, bay leaves, sugar, salt, garlic, and cloves and bring to a boil. Stir occasionally, until the sugar and salt dissolve. Remove from the heat and add the red pepper flakes. Pour the liquid over the vegetables.

Cover and refrigerate overnight. Drain and serve at room temperature.

(To make ahead, store in an airtight container for up to 1 month.)

1 CUP/120 G cauliflower florets

2 large carrots, peeled, cut into ¼-in/6-mm slices

12 radishes, cut into ¼-in/6-mm slices

1 small red onion, cut into ¼-in/6-mm slices

2 jalapeño chiles, coarsely chopped

1½ CUPS/360 ML apple cider vinegar

1½ CUPS/360 ML water

1 TBSP coriander seeds

2 TSP peppercorns

2 bay leaves

¾ CUP/150 G sugar

1 TBSP kosher salt

2 garlic cloves, peeled

1 TSP cloves

1½ TSP red pepper flakes

THE WEST OAKLAND INDUSTRIAL ARTS CORRIDOR

Forklifts and 18-wheelers are as common as cars in West Oakland and it's easy to get the sense that the enormous concrete warehouses here are mere way stations for goods coming in and out of port. What isn't immediately noticeable is that behind the graffiti-strewn walls are dozens of art collectives and studios, and that West Oakland stands as one of the most important centers for industrial arts in the nation. The massive buildings—many are large enough to hold a crane—offer the kind of space artists need to create large-scale installations and sculptures.

American Steel Studios: The two adjacent warehouses here occupy 6 acres and are home to dozens of artists who make everything from 30-foot-high sculptures that weigh close to 30 tons to high-end soap. Fashion designers, glassblowers, fire dancers, and stone carvers share this space that was founded by sculptor Karen Cusolito in 2004.

The Crucible: Imagine a high school shop class gone to Burning Man (in fact many of the artists here head to that festival in Nevada every Labor Day weekend). The Crucible bills itself as an arts education center and offers youth and adult classes in welding, glassblowing, blacksmithing, woodworking, and how to turn a bike into a chariot.

Kinetic Steam Works: You never know what you might see in West Oakland, like maybe a steam engine rolling down the street. That would be *Hortense,* a project of Kinetic Steam Works, an arts organization dedicated to promoting steam-powered technologies, such as a steam-powered printing press, a pumpkin guillotine, and a steamboat the group christened *Wilhelmina.*

St. Louise Studios: Jeremy Crandell, one of Brown Sugar Kitchen's most devoted customers, comes from tech but identifies himself as an arts enabler. In 2007 he founded this studio for industrial artists. With individual studios as well as a shared work floor, innovators have access to the space and tools needed to realize and create large-scale art.

Five-Ton Crane: A retro-futuristic Raygun Gothic Rocketship, an 11,000-pound land-based submarine, a steam-powered treehouse, and a giant hamster wheel for humans designed to run on train tracks are just a few of the projects from this West Oakland–based artist collective.

CHAPTER 5
LARGE PLATES
& BIG BOWLS

We don't serve dinner at Brown Sugar Kitchen. Our doors close at 3 P.M., so lunch is our big meal of the day. During the week we stop making eggs and serving bacon and sausage around 11:30 and roll out the gumbo, catfish, and baby back ribs.

The mood of the restaurant changes, too, once the breakfast rush ends. People are more awake and ready for conversation. The decibel level rises and appetites are bigger. We're more lively in the kitchen, as well.

The line has become a well-oiled machine thanks to devoted cooks and kitchen managers. Some customers ask why we don't smile more when we cook, but getting the food out quickly and doing it well requires a lot of focus. You will find us smiling at the end of the day, when we learn that we served 402 meals in 8 hours, in our little restaurant with just 50 seats, 6 burners, a 3-foot/0.9-metre griddle, and 3 waffle makers. It's truly the little restaurant that could.

Everything at Brown Sugar Kitchen is cooked to order, *à la minute*, as my cooking teachers in France used to say. The only canned items we stock are pineapple juice, plum tomatoes, and evaporated milk. Everything else is made from the raw, fresh state. I think it's hard for people to imagine all of that fresh food coming out of our tiny kitchen; you'd be surprised at how many people are used to food that sits under heat lamps for a long time before it gets to their table. In my kitchen, each piece of fried chicken we serve is juicy and crisp because it just finished cooking. Our highly skilled cooks work efficiently to make each dish to order, but make no mistake, this is slow food.

BUTTERMILK FRIED CHICKEN

When I was growing up, my mother fried chicken at least three times a week. She cooked it in a cast-iron skillet and always used vegetable shortening. The seasoned flour went into a paper bag. She'd drop the chicken pieces in and give them a good shake before frying. I took her fried chicken for granted, assuming it was what everyone was eating. Only later did I learn most of my friends only knew fried chicken as fast food. Years later, when I was working at a restaurant in Manhattan, I discovered a buttermilk-soaked version of fried chicken that rocked my world. That's the way I've made it ever since. The buttermilk bath serves as a tenderizing brine that makes the chicken extra moist and flavorful. You'll notice that I cook the chicken just until crisp in the frying pan and then transfer it to the oven to finish cooking. The skin stays crisp and I know for certain that the meat is cooked through all the way to the bone.

In a large bowl, combine the parsley, tarragon, onion powder, paprika, 2 tsp salt, garlic powder, cayenne, 1 tsp black pepper, oregano, and thyme. Add the chicken pieces and toss to coat. Pour in the buttermilk, cover the bowl with plastic wrap, and refrigerate at least 8 hours or up to overnight.

Preheat the oven to 350°F/180°C. In a large cast-iron frying pan, add oil to a depth of ¾ in/2 cm and heat the oil to 350°F/180°C over medium heat until hot but not smoking. Line a rimmed baking sheet with paper towels and set a wire rack on top.

In a large wide bowl, combine the flour, 1 tbsp salt, and 1 tbsp black pepper. One piece at a time and letting any excess buttermilk drip back into the bowl, transfer the chicken to the flour mixture. Dredge the chicken in the flour mixture, shaking off the excess.

Fry the chicken, a few pieces at a time, taking care not to crowd the pan and turning occasionally, until crisp and browned, 5 to 7 minutes. Transfer to the rack over the baking sheet to continue cooking in the oven until the internal temperature registers 165°F/75°C, about 20 minutes. Remove from the oven and allow to rest for 5 to 10 minutes. Repeat with the remaining chicken. Serve immediately.

2 TBSP minced fresh parsley

1 TBSP dried tarragon

1 TBSP onion powder

1 TBSP sweet paprika

2 TSP kosher salt, plus 1 TBSP

2 TSP garlic powder

1 TSP cayenne pepper

1 TSP freshly ground black pepper, plus 1 TBSP

1 TSP dried oregano

1 TSP dried thyme

3½ LB/1.6 KG chicken, cut into 8 pieces

1 CUP/240 ML buttermilk

Canola or rice bran oil for deep-frying

1½ CUPS/185 G all-purpose flour

JERK BABY BACK RIBS WITH PINEAPPLE SALSA

The first time I worked with jerk spices was in the late '90s, when I was the chef at a Caribbean-influenced restaurant in New York City's East Village. I think I first used it on chicken and then I started trying it on seafood, pork, and just about anything, as they do in Jamaica. I love the notes of cinnamon, nutmeg, and allspice, sweet warming spices that most Americans don't expect to find in their savory foods. The key to flavorful ribs is marinating them for at least 24 hours and cooking them slowly while continuing to baste them. As my father says, "You'd be a jerk not to love them."

JERK MARINADE

1 large red onion, cut into ¼-in/6-mm slices

¾ CUP/180 ML soy sauce

¾ CUP/180 ML vegetable oil

½ CUP/120 ML apple cider vinegar

½ CUP/120 ML water

1 jalapeño chile, sliced

HABANERO VINEGAR

½ habanero chile, stemmed and seeded

⅓ CUP/80 ML white wine vinegar

PINEAPPLE GLAZE

TWO 6-oz/180-ml cans pineapple juice

¼ CUP/50 G firmly packed brown sugar

To make the jerk marinade: In a medium bowl, combine the onion, soy sauce, oil, vinegar, water, and jalapeño. (To make ahead, refrigerate in an airtight container for up to 3 days.)

To make the habanero vinegar: In a food processor, combine the habanero chile and vinegar and purée until smooth. Pour into a small bowl. (To make ahead, refrigerate in an airtight container for up to 1 month.)

To make the pineapple glaze: In a small saucepan, combine the pineapple juice and brown sugar. Bring to a boil over medium heat and cook until sauce is thick and reduced to about one-third, about 15 minutes. (To make ahead, refrigerate in an airtight container for up to 3 days.)

To make the pineapple salsa: In a medium bowl, combine the pineapple, onion, jalapeños, bell pepper, cilantro, oil, and lime juice. Season with salt. (To make ahead, refrigerate in an airtight container for up to 8 hours.)

To make the jerk spice rub: In a small bowl, combine the garlic powder, onion powder, allspice, salt, nutmeg, chile powder, cinnamon, cayenne, and black pepper. (To make ahead, store in a cool, dark place for up to 1 month.)

CONTINUED

PINEAPPLE SALSA

½ pineapple, diced

1 small red onion, diced

3 small jalapeño chiles, diced

⅓ CUP/55 G diced red bell pepper

⅓ CUP/8 G chopped fresh cilantro

2 TBSP canola oil

Juice of 1 lime

Kosher salt

JERK SPICE RUB

2 TBSP garlic powder

2 TBSP onion powder

1 TBSP ground allspice

1 TBSP kosher salt

2 TSP grated nutmeg

2 TSP cascabel or ancho chile powder

2 TSP ground cinnamon

2 TSP ground cayenne pepper

1 TSP freshly ground black pepper

TWO 2-lb/910-g racks baby back ribs

Use a butter knife to pry the membrane off the bone side of the ribs. Once you get a piece of the membrane loose, grab it with a paper towel and pull it toward the other end of the slab to remove it. Rub the Jerk Spice Rub evenly over the ribs. Arrange the ribs in a 15-by-10-in/38-by-25-cm baking pan. Pour the Jerk Marinade over the ribs, turning to coat both sides. Cover the baking pan with aluminum foil and refrigerate for at least 6 hours or up to 24 hours.

Remove the ribs from the marinade, letting the excess drip off. Transfer the ribs to a baking sheet and allow to come to room temperature, about 30 minutes. Brush with the Habanero Vinegar.

To cook ribs using a charcoal grill: Prepare the grill for indirect cooking over medium heat. Place a shallow metal pan filled with water in the center of the grill and arrange the hot coals around it. Lightly oil the grill grates. Place the ribs on the grate directly above the water-filled pan, cover the grill, and cook until tender, 1½ to 2 hours. Add coals as needed to maintain medium heat.

To cook ribs using a gas grill: Preheat the grill with all the burners on high. Lightly oil the grill grates. Place the ribs on the grate, turn off the burner directly under the ribs, and reduce the other burners to medium heat. Cover the grill and cook until tender, $1\frac{1}{2}$ to 2 hours.

After 45 minutes, brush the ribs with some of the Pineapple Glaze, and brush them two or three times before serving. Do not flip the ribs during cooking. When the ribs are done, they will be well browned and the meat will have shrunk back from the ends of the bones. Transfer the ribs to a cutting board and let stand for 5 minutes before cutting each rack into individual ribs.

Serve warm with the Pineapple Salsa.

NORTH AFRICAN SPICED BEEF SHORT RIBS

I was introduced to *ras el hanout* when I worked at a French bistro in Boston. Like me, the chef there had spent some time in the south of France, and he couldn't ignore the influence of North African flavors in French cuisine. Just across the Mediterranean Sea from the Moroccan, Algerian, and Tunisian borders, the south of France is filled with expatriates from these countries. And they bring their flavors with them. I was seduced by a complex combination of spices—allspice, cumin, cardamom, cloves, turmeric, and more. It was like nothing I ever tasted before. It reminds me of an East Indian curry, in that every household has its own recipe. The flavors are bold enough to stands up to the richness of a thick-cut braised meat. Keep consistent with the Moroccan theme and serve these with warm couscous.

2 TBSP minced garlic

1 TBSP grated fresh ginger

2 jalapeño chiles, sliced

¾ CUP/180 ML canola oil

½ CUP/120 ML soy sauce

5 LB/2.3 KG beef short ribs, cut into 2-in/5-cm pieces

Ras el Hanout (facing page)

6 CUPS/1.4 L chicken stock

2 yellow onions, cut into large dice

3 stalks celery, cut into large dice

3 large carrots, peeled and cut into large dice

½ CUP/65 G dried apricots

¼ CUP/60 ML mirin

2 TBSP Green Harissa (page 96) or store-bought harissa

In a bowl or roasting pan large enough to hold the ribs, combine the garlic, ginger, jalapeños, oil, and soy sauce. Add the ribs and toss well to coat. Cover the bowl with plastic wrap and refrigerate for at least 6 hours or up to 24 hours.

Preheat the oven to 325°F/165°C. Remove the ribs from their marinade, letting the excess drip off, and use a fork or your fingers to pick out the jalapeño slices from the marinade to reserve. Transfer the ribs to a large plate or baking sheet, and allow to come to room temperature, about 30 minutes.

Rub the ras el hanout evenly over the ribs. Place the ribs in a Dutch oven large enough to hold them and the stock without overflowing. Add the stock, onions, celery, carrots, apricots, mirin, harissa, and the chiles reserved from the marinade. Bring to a boil, reduce to a simmer, cover, and cook until the ribs are quite tender and the meat pulls easily from the bone, about 2½ hours. Serve immediately.

(To make ahead, refrigerate the ribs in their braising liquid for up to 5 days. Reheat gently in a 325°F/165°C oven or on top of the stove over low heat.)

RAS EL HANOUT

In an electric spice or coffee grinder or with a mortar and pestle, grind or crush the allspice, cumin, peppercorns, cardamom, cayenne, cinnamon, cloves, coriander seeds, ginger, mace, nutmeg, turmeric, thyme, and bay leaf. (To make ahead, store in an airtight container for up to 1 month.)

½ **TSP whole allspice**

½ **TSP cumin seeds**

1 **TSP peppercorns**

½ **TSP ground cardamom**

¼ **TSP cayenne pepper**

½ **TSP ground cinnamon**

¼ **TSP ground cloves**

¾ **TSP toasted coriander seeds (see page 75)**

¼ **TSP ground ginger**

¼ **TSP ground mace**

¼ **TSP grated nutmeg**

¾ **TSP turmeric**

¼ **TSP dried thyme**

1 **bay leaf**

BLACKENED STEAK
AU POIVRE

When I was first taking cooking classes in the late '80s, I was the best student I'd ever been. I couldn't get enough of food—tasting it, reading about it, discovering new combinations of flavors and ingredients. And I particularly loved learning new cooking techniques. The searing, deglazing, and reducing required to make a proper steak au poivre was one that I loved to practice. My favorite cut of steak for this recipe is a boneless rib-eye, but tenderloin and New York strip also work well.

BLACKENING SPICE
1 TSP kosher salt
1 TSP sweet paprika
1 TSP onion powder
¾ TSP garlic powder
½ TSP freshly ground pepper
½ TSP dried oregano
½ TSP dried thyme

TWO 12-oz/340-g rib-eye steaks, cut in half
1 TBSP canola oil
¼ CUP/60 ML sherry
¼ CUP/60 ML beef or chicken stock
¼ CUP/60 ML heavy cream

To make the blackening spice: In a small bowl, combine the salt, paprika, onion powder, garlic powder, black pepper, oregano, and thyme.

Rub the spice mixture evenly over the steaks.

In a cast-iron skillet or sauté pan, heat the oil over medium-high heat until shimmering. Add the steaks and cook to desired doneness, about 3 minutes per side, or until a meat thermometer stuck into the center of the steaks reaches 120°F/48°C for rare, or 130°F/55°C for medium-rare. Transfer the steaks to a serving plate and cover with aluminum foil.

Add the sherry and stock to the skillet and bring to a boil, scraping any browned bits off the bottom of the pan. Stir in the cream and any collected juices from the serving plate, reduce to a simmer, and cook until thickened. Spoon sauce over the steaks. Serve immediately.

CREOLE
MEATLOAF

Let's face it, meatloaf is a good thing. And when it's seasoned with a blend of herbes de Provence, cumin, and cayenne like this one, it's even better than you remember. Just ask Greg "call me if you're serving meatloaf," one of this dish's most avid fans. If you're used to meatloaf in a loaf pan, I urge you to try this free-form method, which allows a delicious crust to develop on the sides as well as the top. Any leftover meatloaf makes a terrific sandwich; I like mine with Spicy Green Coleslaw (page 82) and Pickled Vegetables (page 129).

Preheat the oven to 350°F/180°C.

In a large bowl, use your hands to gently combine the beef, Creole Spice Mix, eggs, bread crumbs, onion, garlic, and ketchup, taking care not to overwork the meat. Shape into an oblong loaf about 9 in/23 cm long and 5 in/12 cm wide. Place in a large roasting pan.

To make the glaze: In a small bowl, combine the herbes de Provence and the ketchup. Brush the meatloaf with half of the glaze.

Bake for 30 minutes, then coat with the remaining glaze. Continue baking until a meat thermometer stuck into the center of the meatloaf registers 160°F/70°C, 20 to 30 minutes more.

Allow the meatloaf to rest for 10 minutes before slicing. Serve warm.

(To make ahead, cover the cooked meatloaf with plastic wrap or aluminum foil and refrigerate for up to 3 days. Reheat in a 325°F/165°C oven until warmed through.)

2½ LB/1.2 KG lean ground beef
¼ CUP/35 G Creole Spice Mix (page 51)
3 eggs, beaten
1 CUP/55 G fresh bread crumbs
1 large yellow onion, diced
4 garlic cloves, minced
¾ CUP/220 G ketchup

GLAZE
1 TBSP herbes de Provence
½ CUP/150 G ketchup

SHRIMP & CHICKEN GUMBO

My mother and her three sisters all grew up in the same household in Louisiana, but they all cook different versions of gumbo. I make a version slightly different from the one my mom makes, a tomato and okra combination with lots of shrimp and chicken. I leave out the tomatoes and add a dark roux like my aunt Maxine. She prefers a dark roux to cradle the oysters that she loves so much. Aunt Essie still lives in Shreveport and takes advantage of she-crab when it's in season. And then there's my aunt Martha Ray, who frankly doesn't cook much but loves to eat gumbo no matter who makes it.

Preheat the oven to 300°F/150°C. Cut the garlic in half widthwise and put both halves on a sheet of aluminum foil. Drizzle with the olive oil, and season with salt and pepper. Wrap tightly in the foil and roast until the garlic is tender, about 1 hour.

In a heavy-bottomed pot, heat the 1 cup/240 ml vegetable oil over medium-high heat until very hot and almost smoking. Add the flour and cook, stirring constantly, until the roux is a deep caramel color, about 5 minutes. Set aside.

In a large soup pot, heat the remaining 1 tbsp oil over medium-low heat. Add the celery, bell pepper, and onion and cook until the vegetables are quite soft, about 20 minutes. Squeeze the roasted garlic cloves out of their skins and add to the pot, along with the stock. Bring to a boil, reduce to a simmer, and whisk in the roux. Cook until the gumbo base begins to thicken, about 10 minutes. Stir in the Creole Spice Mix and the gumbo filé powder. Add the okra and cook until the okra is tender, about 10 minutes. Add the chicken and the shrimp and cook just until the shrimp is opaque in the center, about 5 minutes. Taste and season with salt and pepper.

Serve immediately over rice, if desired.

(To make ahead, refrigerate the gumbo in an airtight container for up to 3 days. Reheat in a saucepan over medium heat.)

1 head garlic

½ TSP olive oil

Kosher salt and freshly ground pepper

1 CUP/240 ML vegetable oil, plus 1 TBSP

1 CUP/125 G all-purpose flour

2 stalks celery, diced

1 green bell pepper, diced

1 large yellow onion, diced

8 CUPS/2 L chicken stock

1½ TSP Creole Spice Mix (page 51)

1½ TSP gumbo filé powder

1 LB/455 G okra, trimmed and cut into ½-in/12-mm rounds

2 LB/910 G cooked chicken, shredded

2 LB/910 G medium shrimp, peeled and deveined

Cooked rice for serving (optional)

BAYOUBAISSE

My first job after cooking school was an unpaid *stage* at a Michelin-starred restaurant in a Relais Chateaux resort hotel on the island of Porquerolles. Just off the coast near St. Tropez, this region is considered part of Provence, my favorite area of France. It was like a dream: black sand on one side, white sand on the other—not to mention the delicious seafood. That's when I learned there's nothing quite like a chilled Provençal rosé on a hot summer day. And it's a perfect match for bayoubaisse—my Creole-inspired riff on the famous bouillabaisse, a seafood stew that's synonymous with the south of France.

2 TBSP canola oil

2 medium yellow onions, diced

2 leeks, white parts only, washed and diced

4 garlic cloves, minced

2 stalks celery, diced

1 fennel bulb, diced

2 carrots, peeled and diced

6 Roma tomatoes, chopped

1 TBSP tomato paste

1 CUP/240 ML dry white wine

8 CUPS/2 L chicken stock

4 CUPS/960 ML water

¾ TSP ground cumin

½ TSP cayenne pepper

½ TSP smoked paprika

¼ TSP dried thyme

¼ TSP dried marjoram

Kosher salt and freshly ground black pepper

1 LB/455 G Atlantic cod fillet

3 bay leaves

8 OZ/225 G new potatoes, quartered

12 clams or mussels (or both)

In a large heavy-bottomed pot, heat the oil over medium-high heat until shimmering. Add the onions, leeks, garlic, celery, fennel, carrots, and Roma tomatoes and cook, stirring occasionally, until softened, about 15 minutes. Stir in the tomato paste, wine, stock, water, cumin, cayenne, paprika, thyme, marjoram, 1½ tsp salt, and 1 tsp black pepper. Bring to a boil, reduce to a simmer, and cook until the vegetables are quite soft, about 30 minutes Add the cod and continue simmering until the fish falls apart, about 15 minutes.

If using an immersion blender, turn off the heat and process the soup until well combined but still chunky. If using a standing blender or food processor, let the broth cool slightly and blend on medium speed until well combined but still chunky. Return the liquid to the stockpot.

1½ LB/680 G striped bass or red snapper, cut into 2-in/5-cm pieces

12 medium shrimp, peeled and deveined

1 CUP/150 G cherry or grape tomatoes, halved

4 OZ/115 G sourdough baguette, cut into 6 slices and toasted

Chopped fresh herbs, such as chives, parsley, and fennel fronds, for garnish

Increase the heat to medium, add the bay leaves and potatoes, and simmer until the potatoes are tender, about 20 minutes. Add the clams and cook until they open, 5 to 7 minutes. Add the striped bass, shrimp, and cherry tomatoes and cook just until the shrimp is opaque, about 3 minutes. Season with salt and pepper.

Garnish with the sourdough toast and chopped fresh herbs. Serve immediately.

BLACKENED CATFISH

Responsibly farmed catfish, like the kind we serve at Brown Sugar Kitchen, are a "best choice" on the Monterey Bay Aquarium Seafood Watch list. Catfish is very delicate, and not a good choice for grilling, but perfect for this preparation. I think its slightly sweet flavor is a great foil for some spice and this blackening spice definitely has a kick. Get out your cast-iron skillet and get real. Nothing tastes better with this dish than sweet corn and in-season tomatoes.

In a heavy-bottomed saucepan, combine the rice with the water. Cook, uncovered, over high heat until steam holes appear on the surface of the rice. Reduce the heat to very low, cover the pan, and cook for 15 minutes. Remove from the heat and let stand, covered, for 5 minutes. Add the Creole Spice Mix, parsley, 1 tbsp of the butter, and the salt to the rice and fluff with a fork. Cover and set aside.

Coat the catfish fillets evenly with the blackening spice. In a cast-iron frying pan, heat the oil over medium-high heat until shimmering. Add the catfish and cook until the bottoms are browned, about 2 minutes. Carefully turn the catfish over and add the remaining 1 tbsp butter, the garlic, lemon juice, and thyme. Cook, taking a spoon and pouring the juices over the catfish once or twice, until the catfish is browned and flakes easily, about 2 minutes.

Place the fish fillets on individual plates. Stir any remaining pan juices into the rice, and spoon the rice alongside the fish. Drizzle with the Roasted Red Pepper Sauce. Serve immediately.

1 CUP/215 G long-grain white rice

1 CUP/240 ML water

¼ TSP Creole Spice Mix (page 51)

1 TBSP minced fresh parsley

2 TBSP unsalted butter

½ TSP kosher salt

FOUR 6-oz/170-g catfish fillets

1 TBSP Blackening Spice (page 144)

1 TBSP canola oil

2 garlic cloves, minced

1 TBSP fresh lemon juice

2 sprigs fresh thyme

¼ CUP/60 ML Roasted Red Pepper Sauce (page 152)

ROASTED RED PEPPER SAUCE

ONE 15-oz/430-g jar roasted red bell peppers

2 garlic cloves, minced

2 DASHES of Tabasco sauce, plus more as needed

Kosher salt

Drain the peppers, reserving the liquid. In a blender, combine the roasted peppers and ¼ cup/60 ml of their liquid, the garlic, and Tabasco sauce and process until smooth. Taste and season with Tabasco sauce and salt. (To make ahead, refrigerate in an airtight container for up to 1 week.)

BOURBON & CHILI-GLAZED SALMON

Fresh wild salmon definitely qualifies as a splurge, but it's one I indulge in as often as I can during the season, which runs from May to October. The fish requires careful cooking to maintain its succulent flavor. As soon as the milky white juices appear on the surface, it's done. Alvin, a neightbor to our restaurant B-Side Barbecue, eats this dish several times a week. He's a testament to the power of our consistency. The flavor of salmon is more intense than other fish varieties, so it can handle this boldly flavored glaze. We serve it with a simple mixed green salad.

In a small bowl, combine the honey, bourbon, chili powder, ginger, pepper, salt, lime zest, and lime juice.

Preheat the broiler and position the oven rack 6 in/15 cm below the broiler element. Line a baking sheet with aluminum foil. Put the salmon fillets, skin-side down, on the prepared baking sheet and spoon the glaze evenly over them. Broil, without turning, until the glaze is bubbling and salmon is no longer opaque in the center, about 8 minutes. Serve immediately.

¼ CUP/85 G **honey**

1½ TBSP **bourbon**

2 TBSP **chili powder**

½ TSP **ground ginger**

¼ TSP **freshly ground pepper**

¼ TSP **salt**

½ TSP **lime zest**

Juice of ½ **lime**

FOUR 6-oz/170-g **skin-on salmon fillets**

B-SIDE BBQ
BRAISED SMOKED TOFU WITH
ROASTED EGGPLANT

Some customers laugh when they see this tofu on the menu, as if to question why anyone other than a strict vegetarian would choose it over ribs. Well, one bite and they reconsider. At B-Side, we're fortunate to be able to source our tofu from Hodo Soy Beanery, a producer based here in Oakland, which makes a meaty, organic tofu that really takes on the flavor of the sauce.

In a large bowl, combine the salt, paprika, garlic powder, onion powder, cayenne, black pepper, oregano, and thyme. Add the tofu and toss to coat, rubbing the spices over the tofu if needed.

Ignite an electric grill and set to 200°F/95°C, or start a small fire in a charcoal grill. If using an electric grill, place hickory, mesquite, or any other aromatic wood chips in a piece of aluminum foil and punch holes in the foil with a fork. Set the foil package on top of the grill grates. (If using a charcoal grill, place the wood chips directly on the charcoal.) Put the tofu on the grate, cover the grill, and cook until the tofu is infused with the flavor of the smoke, 25 to 30 minutes.

Preheat the oven to 400°F/200°C. Line a baking sheet with parchment paper. In a large bowl, combine the eggplant, olive oil, and salt and toss until evenly coated. Spread the eggplant in a single layer on the prepared baking sheet, and bake until tender, about 20 minutes.

Meanwhile, in a large saucepan, combine the barbecue sauce and water. Bring to a boil, reduce to a simmer, and cook until the mixture begins to thicken, about 30 minutes.

Add the smoked tofu and the roasted eggplant to the pan, and let simmer until the tofu and the eggplant are infused with the flavor of the sauce, about 25 minutes. Serve immediately.

½ TSP kosher salt

½ TSP hot paprika

¼ TSP garlic powder

½ TSP onion powder

¼ TSP cayenne pepper

¼ TSP freshly ground black pepper

¼ TSP dried oregano

¼ TSP dried thyme

1½ LB/680 G firm tofu, cut into ¾-in/2-cm cubes

2 eggplants, cut into ¾-in/2-cm cubes

3 TBSP olive oil

1 TSP kosher salt

1½ CUPS/360 ML Molasses BBQ Sauce (page 156)

3 CUPS/720 ML water

MOLASSES BBQ SAUCE

1 TBSP unsalted butter

1 red onion, minced

6 garlic cloves, minced

1 TBSP grated fresh ginger

1 TBSP Dijon mustard

¼ CUP/60 ML apple cider vinegar

2 TBSP soy sauce

½ CUP/100 G firmly packed brown sugar

2 TBSP ketchup

1½ TBSP Worcestershire sauce

1 TBSP fresh lemon juice

1 TBSP canned chipotle chiles in adobo

2½ TSP chile powder

1½ CUPS/285 G chopped canned peeled plum tomatoes

¼ CUP/60 ML molasses

Kosher salt and freshly ground pepper

In a large heavy-bottomed saucepan, melt the butter over medium heat. Add the onion, garlic, and ginger and cook until the onion starts to soften, about 10 minutes. Stir in the mustard, vinegar, soy sauce, sugar, ketchup, Worcestershire sauce, lemon juice, chipotle chiles, and chile powder and continue cooking for 10 minutes more.

Add the tomatoes with their juice and molasses and cook until the sauce is thick and flavorful, about 30 minutes.

Transfer to a blender or food processor and process until smooth. Season with salt and pepper. (To make ahead, refrigerate in an airtight container for up to 2 months.)

BOOTS RILEY

MUSICIAN, FRONT MAN FOR STREET SWEEPER SOCIAL CLUB AND THE COUP, COMMUNITY ACTIVIST

Lives: West Oakland, since 2006

Regular order: Shrimp and grits

People associated me with West Oakland long before I lived here. The Coup and Street Sweeper Social Club shot a lot of videos in the neighborhood. Whenever a producer comes from the East Coast they want to shoot here. They like the architecture—the old buildings and the old houses. I moved to Lower Bottoms in 2006 and it's the friendliest neighborhood I've ever lived in. Families that moved here in the 1950s and '60s are still here. Someone will say, "Oh, it's a sunny day. Let's have a barbecue on the sidewalk." If someone doesn't show up, they go knock on their door and say, "Hey, you didn't get a plate," and offer some food. I had a studio at Tenth Street and Wood Street filled with tens of thousands of dollars' worth of equipment. Often I would be in such a rush that I'd leave my door open all day, but nothing was ever taken. That's the benefit of community and people knowing each other. When we were recording our last album we came to Brown Sugar Kitchen every day. The studio was just a few blocks away, and we would come for coffee and pastry in the mornings and sometimes later for a meal. The people in West Oakland are really proud of Brown Sugar Kitchen. Like the neighborhood, it's a remix of the old and the new. Because the food represents black culture, the people here see it as a beacon. It's part of the ideal of what West Oakland should be.

THE SOUND OF WEST OAKLAND

Music, like food, can forge community. It soothes the rough edges that keep people apart and feeds a common need. In West Oakland, music has a long history of bringing people together. In the 1940s, the neighborhood was known as the Harlem of the West, attracting artists like Billie Holiday, Big Mama Thornton, and Aretha Franklin to the clubs that lined Seventh Street. Faded signs for famous venues like Esther's Orbit Room and Slim Jenkins can still be seen on the facades on the buildings there. Decades later, in the 1990s, D'wayne Wiggins, who was born in the Lower Bottom in West Oakland, brought fresh attention to the area when he opened House of Music on Wood Street and brought artists like Destiny's Child, India Arie, and Jamie Foxx in to record. His own group, Tony! Toni! Toné!, continues to tour. Today the neighborhood is home to musicians like Boots Riley and Al Lucchesi's Soundwave Studios, where Third Eye Blind, metal bands like Testament, and the late Tupac Shakur have all recorded. Musicians know they have a home at Brown Sugar Kitchen, where they drop by during breaks in their sessions for a cup of coffee or a meal. Their music feeds our souls. We can only hope to return the favor with a plate of chicken and waffles.

KOFY BROWN

MUSICIAN

Lives: West Oakland, since 1994

Regular order: Beignets

I met Tanya at a party shortly after she and Phil moved to West Oakland. She told me she was going to open a restaurant in the neighborhood. When Brown Sugar Kitchen opened, I didn't know it was hers until I walked in and saw her cooking. Now I eat here about once a week. West Oakland has a buzz; there's a spirit and I can feel it. I've lived here long enough to see attitudes transformed. I chose to live here because it's an industrial neighborhood. It's cool. The people are impassioned. It's a perfect place to build a community. There's a mix of incomes but people have a shared vision and they look out for each other. West Oakland has a history of people pulling together. This community has a spark and when you live here you start to appreciate it. It's a real melting pot, true diversity. What we have here is rare. People talk to each other, not to say, "Be like me," but to say, "Who are you, what are you doing?"

ALAN LUCCHESI

OWNER, SOUNDWAVE STUDIOS

Works: West Oakland, since 1992

Regular order: Beignets

My house burned down in the Oakland hills fire in 1991, and we got enough money out of the insurance deal to buy a building here. We came because it's on the edge of town and there's no one to bother us. We have a lot of elbow room here and not much supervision. We can do what we want. People feel like they can relax here. It's not an uptight place to be. After the freeway came down, this area opened up. When I moved here people thought I was nuts, but musicians are loud, we can't go just anywhere. West Oakland is a great location for us. At the studio, we'll have a mariachi band in one room, someone rapping in another, and someone doing techno down the hall. It's a mash-up of people who would never meet anyplace else and they're all hanging out together. It's a microcosm of this area. Everyone is in harmony. Now I'm trying to open a club, but first I had to convince the city that it was a good idea. When Tanya and Phil wrote us a recommendation, the doors at City Hall blew open. They are very enamored of Brown Sugar Kitchen there. One of the planning commissioners said, "If Brown Sugar Kitchen thinks it's a good idea, I'm in."

CHAPTER 6
SWEETS

Southerners are known to have a sweet tooth, and even though I was born in Connecticut, I inherited the gene. My Southern grandmothers were both home bakers and there was always a cake or pie on their kitchen counters. I grew up attending a traditional Southern Baptist church that would often hold bake sales. Cookies, layer cakes, cobblers, puddings, and pies are part of a long tradition in the soul food kitchen and I love them all.

To my mind, a meal isn't complete until I've had dessert. While I've spent most of my career working on the savory side of the kitchen, there have been several times when I've had to work in the pastry department, and I'm a better cook for the experience. Baking requires more patience and precision of timing and measurement.

A number of bakers have influenced the sweets we offer at Brown Sugar Kitchen. It's perhaps the most challenging job in the restaurant. Our bakers must work in a very small space, sharing the two ovens with the rest of the cooks, and there's very little room in the refrigerator for the storage they need. Still, it's amazing to see what our bakers can do.

When we opened, my friend Tina, who had once owned a bakery, helped get our baking traditions started. She brought her sticky buns to the mix. Next came Shuna, a French Laundry alum, who organized the recipes and translated them into restaurant-quantity numbers. She was followed by Gillian, whose affinity for homemade desserts and jams made people pay attention to the baked goods display. Jeremy took over after Gillian left to start her own bakery. He turned out to have a natural baking talent, but his leadership skills are so exceptional that after a year of baking, we brought him back to the savory side to be our kitchen manager. The petite Lauren took over next. She doesn't look like she's ever eaten cake or cookies, but she has an incredible talent for baking. Some of her best work is in this chapter: the Caramelized Banana Pudding (page 165), Black-Bottom Maple-Pecan Bars (page 173), and Pineapple Upside-Down Cake (page 184) to name a few.

BOURBON-HAZELNUT
TRUFFLES

Bourbon, chocolate, and hazelnuts—need I say more? I first discovered hazelnuts when I was a student at the old Peter Kump's New York Cooking School on Manhattan's Upper East Side. I learned so much that year and I worked with many ingredients that were new to me. We were taught to roast and peel them, and I was so bowled over by their smell that I could barely wait for them to cool before eating them.

½ CUP/55 G hazelnuts, toasted (see page 75)

2 TBSP firmly packed brown sugar

⅔ CUP/165 ML heavy cream

8 OZ/225 G best-quality semisweet or dark chocolate, finely chopped

2 TBSP bourbon

¼ CUP/20 G unsweetened cocoa powder

In a food processor, combine the hazelnuts and brown sugar and grind together until the nuts are uniformly pulverized.

In a medium saucepan, bring the cream to a simmer over medium heat. Remove from the heat and add the chocolate. Let stand, undisturbed, for about 2 minutes, then whisk until the chocolate is completely melted. Stir in the bourbon and hazelnut mixture. Transfer the chocolate mixture to a small bowl, cover with plastic wrap, and refrigerate until thoroughly cold, about 3 hours.

Line a baking sheet with parchment paper. Using a teaspoon and your hands or a small melon baller, form the chocolate into small balls and place on the prepared baking sheet. You should have 24 balls. Cover loosely with plastic wrap and refrigerate until firm, about 1 hour.

Sift the cocoa powder into a small bowl. A few at a time, add the truffles to the bowl, and toss to coat with the cocoa powder. Transfer to a serving plate or place in paper or aluminum foil candy cups. Serve at room temperature.

(To make ahead, refrigerate in an airtight container for up to 1 week.)

CARAMELIZED BANANA PUDDING

Banana pudding is one of my dad's favorite desserts. We always made it with store-bought vanilla wafers using the recipe on the side of the box. At Brown Sugar Kitchen we never make anything from a box, so we developed this recipe, which includes a homemade version of that famous cookie, but the caramelized bananas are the best part of this dish.

To make the vanilla wafers: Preheat the oven to 350°F/180°C. Line a baking sheet with parchment paper.

In a bowl, sift together the flour, baking powder, and salt. Using a stand mixer fitted with the paddle attachment, beat the butter and granulated sugar on medium speed until light and fluffy, about 5 minutes. Reduce the speed to low and add the flour mixture, beating just until crumbly. In a small bowl, combine the vanilla and milk, then slowly pour it into the dough mixture. Beat just until the dough comes together to form a ball.

Place the dough on a clean work surface and roll it into a log about 1 in/2.5 cm wide and about 8 in/20 cm long. Cut the log into ¼-in/6-mm slices and place the slices on the prepared baking sheet about 1 in/2.5 cm apart. You should have about 32 cookies. Bake until the cookie tops are no longer soft to the touch, 12 to 15 minutes. Let cool on the baking sheet for 5 minutes. Transfer to a wire rack to cool completely.

To make the pudding: Set a medium bowl over an ice bath. In a small bowl, whisk together the egg yolks until smooth and pale. In a saucepan over medium heat, whisk together the flour, granulated sugar, and salt, then add the milk and vanilla and whisk until combined. Cook, whisking occasionally, until you see the first big, boiling bubble. Slowly pour the hot milk

CONTINUED

VANILLA WAFERS
¾ CUP/95 G all-purpose flour
¼ TSP baking powder
¼ TSP kosher salt
4 TBSP/60 G unsalted butter, at room temperature
⅓ CUP/65 G granulated sugar
1 TBSP vanilla extract
1 TBSP whole milk

PUDDING
4 egg yolks
½ CUP/60 G all-purpose flour
½ CUP/100 G granulated sugar
¼ TSP kosher salt
3 CUPS/720 ML whole milk
2 TSP vanilla extract

CARAMELIZED BANANAS
4 TBSP/55 G unsalted butter
½ CUP/100 G firmly packed brown sugar
¼ TSP ground cinnamon
¼ TSP kosher salt
4 firm, ripe bananas, sliced

mixture into the bowl with the egg yolks, whisking all the while so as not to scramble the eggs. Transfer this mixture back to the saucepan, and cook over medium-low heat, whisking often, until thickened, about 5 minutes. Strain the pudding through a fine-mesh sieve into the bowl in the ice bath. Immediately press a piece of plastic wrap directly onto the surface of the pudding to keep a skin from forming. Let cool completely. Refrigerate until ready to assemble the puddings.

To make the caramelized bananas: In a wide sauté pan, heat the butter, brown sugar, cinnamon, and salt over medium heat, stirring occasionally, until the butter melts, the sugar dissolves, and the mixture bubbles, 2 to 3 minutes. Add the banana slices and, using a spoon, turn gently to coat the slices with the sugar mixture until the bananas are warmed through and glazed and the sauce thins out, about 3 minutes.

In six 1-cup/240-ml serving cups, layer pudding, 3 vanilla wafers, and about 2 tbsp of the caramelized bananas, then repeat the layers, dividing the ingredients evenly among the cups. Top with cookies.

Serve immediately or cover with plastic wrap and refrigerate until ready to serve. The pudding will keep up to 24 hours, although the cookies will soften.

BUTTERMILK CORNBREAD PUDDING

There's nothing like piping hot cornbread fresh out of the oven and slathered with butter. Leftover cornbread is never quite the same; reheating cold cornbread usually just dries it out (though leftovers do make great croutons; see my Vidalia Onion Soup on page 116). This rich bread pudding will have you craving leftovers. One of our regular customers tells me this reminds him of the cornbread crumbled into a bowl of milk that he ate instead of cereal when he was a kid. I would eat this pudding for dessert, for breakfast, or at any time of day!

3 CUPS/720 ML buttermilk

¾ CUP/150 G sugar

5 eggs plus 3 egg yolks

2 TSP vanilla extract

1 CUP/85 G coarsely crumbled Buttermilk Cornbread (page 106) or corn muffins

½ CUP/70 G dried currants or raisins

Preheat the oven to 425°F/220°C. Butter an 8-by-8-in/20-by-20-cm baking dish.

In a large bowl, whisk together the buttermilk, sugar, eggs, egg yolks, and vanilla. Gently stir in the crumbled cornbread and currants.

Pour the pudding mixture into the prepared baking dish and cover the dish with aluminum foil. Set the baking dish in a roasting pan and fill the pan with enough hot tap water to reach halfway up the sides of the baking dish.

Bake for 1 hour. Remove the foil and bake for 15 minutes more, until the top of the pudding is golden brown. Serve warm or at room temperature.

(To make ahead, cover with aluminum foil and refrigerate for up to 2 days. Reheat, covered, in a 350°F/180°C oven just until heated through, about 20 minutes.)

BEIGNETS WITH CHOCOLATE-CHICORY SAUCE

I can't re-create the atmosphere at Café du Monde, a more-than-a-century-old, open-air coffee shop in New Orleans' French Quarter, but I was inspired by their signature beignets to make my own at Brown Sugar Kitchen. I use a lighter vegetable oil to fry them and a little less powdered sugar than they do at the Café. The chocolate-chicory sauce is my own spin on Café du Monde's signature coffee drink. These are at their best served warm.

To make the sauce: Put the chocolate in a medium heat-proof bowl. In a small saucepan, combine the cream, coffee, and cinnamon stick and bring to a simmer over medium heat. Pour the hot cream mixture over the chocolate. Let stand, undisturbed, for about 2 minutes. Discard the cinnamon stick, then whisk until the chocolate is completely melted and the mixture is blended and smooth. Keep in a warm place while you make the beignets.

To make the beignets: In a small bowl, combine the yeast, granulated sugar, and water. Let stand until foamy, about 5 minutes.

Using a stand mixer fitted with the paddle attachment, combine the eggs, evaporated milk, and salt and mix on medium speed. Stir in the yeast mixture and the melted butter. Reduce the speed to low, add half the flour, and mix just until combined. (Alternately, stir in the flour with a wooden spoon.) Scrape down the sides of the bowl, and add the remaining flour. Continue to mix on low speed until the dough forms a smooth yet slightly sticky ball.

Transfer the dough to an oiled bowl, cover with plastic wrap, and let rise in a warm place until doubled in size, about 1 hour. Punch down the dough. (To make ahead, refrigerate the dough for up to 24 hours. Let come to room temperature for no more than 30 minutes before frying.)

CONTINUED

CHOCOLATE-CHICORY SAUCE

10 OZ/280 G bittersweet chocolate, finely chopped

1½ CUPS/360 ML heavy cream

½ CUP/120 ML brewed chicory coffee, such as Café du Monde brand

1 cinnamon stick

BEIGNETS

2¼ TSP active dry yeast

¼ CUP/50 G granulated sugar

¼ CUP/60 ML warm water

3 eggs, beaten

ONE 12-oz/360-ml can evaporated milk

1 TSP salt

4 TBSP/55 G unsalted butter, melted

3¾ CUPS/470 G all-purpose flour

Canola oil for deep-frying

1 CUP/100 G powdered sugar

1 TSP ground cinnamon

In a large saucepan, add oil to a depth of 1½ in/4 cm. Heat the oil to 365°F/185°C over medium heat until hot but not smoking. While the oil heats, in a small bowl, stir together the powdered sugar and ground cinnamon. Line a baking sheet with paper towels.

Working in batches and taking care not to crowd the pan, drop the dough by the tablespoonful into the hot oil and fry until light gold, about 3 minutes, turning after 1 to 2 minutes. Using a slotted spoon, transfer the beignets to the prepared baking sheet to drain for 30 seconds. Dredge in the cinnamon sugar. Serve hot, with chocolate-chicory sauce for dipping.

CRUNCHY PEANUT BUTTER COOKIES

This is my ultimate comfort cookie. It just begs for a big glass of cold milk or a cup of hot coffee. It's such a simple recipe. I think it was one of the first that I learned in a home economics class in junior high.

1¼ CUPS/155 G all-purpose flour

¼ TSP kosher salt

½ TSP baking soda

½ TSP baking powder

½ CUP/115 G unsalted butter, at room temperature

½ CUP/100 G granulated sugar

½ CUP/100 G firmly packed brown sugar

1 egg

½ CUP/115 G crunchy peanut butter

½ TSP vanilla extract

¼ CUP/50 G raw or turbinado sugar

Preheat the oven to 350°F/180°C. Line a baking sheet with parchment paper.

In a large bowl, stir together the flour, salt, baking soda, and baking powder. Using a stand mixer fitted with the paddle attachment, combine the butter with the granulated and brown sugars and beat on medium speed, scraping the bowl occasionally, until light and fluffy, 2 to 3 minutes. Add the egg and mix until just combined. Add the peanut butter and vanilla and beat until fully incorporated, about 1 minute. Reduce the speed to low, add the flour mixture, and mix until just combined.

Roll the dough into walnut-size balls. You should have about 30 balls. Pour the raw sugar into a shallow dish. Roll the balls in the raw sugar and place on the prepared baking sheet about 2 in/5 cm apart.

Bake until the cookies are just starting to brown, 8 to 10 minutes. Let cool on the baking sheet for 10 minutes. Transfer to a wire rack to cool completely.

(To make ahead, store in an airtight container for up to 2 days.)

BLACK-BOTTOM
MAPLE-PECAN BARS

Sometimes a slice of pecan pie is just too much after a meal of chicken and waffles or a bowl of shrimp and grits, so we came up with these bars that are only slightly less indulgent. I like a little chocolate with my pecan pie, so we bake these on a chocolate crust. Slice them into bite-size pieces to serve as petit fours, or cut them the size of a standard brownie for a more substantial dessert. After noon, wash them down with a glass of bourbon.

To make the crust: Preheat the oven to 350°F/180°C. Butter and flour an 8-in/20-cm square baking pan.

In a food processor, pulse together the flour, cocoa powder, sugar, and salt. Scatter the chilled butter cubes over the flour mixture and pulse until the mixture resembles coarse crumbs. Do not overprocess; the dough will look very dry and crumbly.

Press the dough into the prepared pan evenly across the bottom and about 1 in/2.5 cm up the sides; it should be about ½ in/12 mm thick. Bake until the crust looks dry and slightly puffed, about 15 minutes.

To make the filling: In a small saucepan, combine the butter, brown sugar, maple syrup, and salt and cook over medium-low heat, stirring occasionally, until the butter is melted and the sugar is dissolved. Stir in the pecans and cream, reduce to a simmer, and cook until bubbling and warmed through, about 3 minutes.

When the crust is done, gently press down on any puffed-up areas. Pour the filling evenly over the crust. Bake until the filling has thickened and is bubbling, about 15 minutes. Let cool completely.

Cut into nine squares and serve at room temperature.

(To make ahead, store in an airtight container at room temperature or in the refrigerator for up to 3 days.)

COCOA CRUST

1 CUP/125 G all-purpose flour

¼ CUP/20 G Dutch-processed cocoa powder, sifted

⅓ CUP/65 G firmly packed light brown sugar

¼ TSP kosher salt

½ CUP/115 G unsalted butter, cut into cubes and chilled

PECAN FILLING

6 TBSP/85 G unsalted butter

½ CUP/100 G firmly packed dark brown sugar

2 TBSP pure maple syrup

½ TSP kosher salt

8 OZ/225 G pecans, coarsely chopped

¼ CUP/60 ML heavy cream

PEACH & NECTARINE COBBLER

I remember Grandma Holland was always putting up peaches during the summer so that we could have peach cobbler year-round. If you do that, this can be one of the fastest desserts to make, with a little bit of planning. All you have to do is open a jar of home-canned fruit, add the warm spices, and top with the cobbler dough. Serve it warm with ice cream, please!

Preheat the oven to 375°F/190°C. Butter a 13-by-9-in/33-by-23-cm glass or ceramic baking dish.

In a food processor, combine the flour, baking powder, and salt. Scatter the chilled butter cubes over the flour mixture and pulse until the mixture resembles coarse crumbs. Do not overprocess. Transfer the flour mixture to a large bowl and add ½ cup/100 g of the sugar and the cream, mixing with a wooden spoon just until the dough comes together. Cover the bowl with a kitchen towel and let rest while preparing the filling.

Bring a large pot of water to a boil. Using a paring knife, cut a small "X" into the skin of the peaches and nectarines. Drop the peaches and nectarines into boiling water. As soon as the "X" curls away from the fruits, about 40 seconds, remove them from the water with tongs or a slotted spoon. When cool enough to handle, pull the skin away from the flesh and cut the peaches and nectarines into ½-in-/12-mm-thick slices.

In a large bowl, toss the peach and nectarine slices with the cornstarch, the remaining ¼ cup/50 g sugar, cinnamon, and nutmeg. Spoon the fruit into the prepared baking dish. Cover the fruit with heaping tablespoons of the cobbler dough.

Bake for 35 minutes, until the cobbler is lightly browned and the fruit is bubbling. Let rest for 10 minutes before serving warm.

2 CUPS/255 G all-purpose flour

1 TBSP baking powder

½ TSP kosher salt

½ CUP/115 G unsalted butter, cut into cubes and chilled

¾ CUP/150 G sugar

1 CUP/240 ML heavy cream

3 peaches

3 nectarines

2 TBSP cornstarch

½ TSP ground cinnamon

PINCH of grated nutmeg

COCONUT CHESS TART

Chess pie is an underrated yet wonderful dessert. The traditional version is a rich vanilla-scented custard, though I've had lemon ones as well. I like it with coconut for a bit of tropical flavor. I often prefer a tart to a pie since it's shallower and has a more even ratio of crust to filling.

TART CRUST

2¼ CUPS/285 G all-purpose flour

1 CUP/225 G unsalted butter, cut into cubes and chilled

1 TSP kosher salt

4 TO 7 TBSP/60 TO 105 ML ice water

COCONUT CHESS FILLING

8 TBSP/115 G unsalted butter, at room temperature

2 CUPS/400 G granulated sugar

7 egg yolks

1 CUP/95 G sweetened flaked coconut

1½ TSP vanilla extract

½ CUP/120 ML heavy cream

3 TBSP cornmeal

Powdered sugar for serving

To make the crust: In a food processor, combine the flour, chilled butter, and salt. Pulse until the mixture resembles small peas. Add 4 tbsp/60 ml of the ice water and pulse just until the dough holds together when pressed between your fingers. If necessary, add more water, 1 tbsp at a time. Do not overprocess.

Turn out the dough onto a lightly floured surface. Knead lightly, form into a disk, and wrap with plastic wrap. Refrigerate for at least 30 minutes or up to overnight.

On a lightly floured surface, roll the dough into a ⅛-in-/4-mm-thick circle, slightly larger than a 10-in/25-cm tart pan. Fit the dough into the pan and trim excess from the edges. Refrigerate for at least 30 minutes before filling.

Preheat the oven to 350°F/180°C.

To make the filling: Using a stand mixer fitted with the paddle attachment, cream the butter and sugar on medium speed until light and fluffy, about 3 minutes, scraping down the bowl at least twice. Add the egg yolks, coconut, vanilla, and cream and mix until combined. Stir in the cornmeal.

Pour the filling into the crust and bake until browned and set in the center, 35 to 40 minutes. Shake it a little; the filling should jiggle, but not be too loose.

Transfer to a wire rack to let cool completely. Dust with powdered sugar and slice into wedges. Serve at room temperature.

(To make ahead, cover with plastic wrap and refrigerate for up to 2 days.)

DOWN-HOME
SWEET POTATO
PIE

Sweet potato pie is the only item on the Brown Sugar Kitchen dessert menu that we serve every day. We've played with different crusts, and we think that this one offers just the right amount of tenderness and flakiness. I've toned down the filling so that it's not overly sweet. We put it out on the pastry counter first thing in the morning and you'd be surprised how many of our customers eat it for breakfast.

To make the crust: In a medium bowl, combine the flour, baking powder, and salt. Add the chilled butter and use a pastry cutter or two knives to cut the butter into the flour until the mixture resembles coarse crumbs. Add the sour cream and stir just until the dough comes together.

Turn out the dough onto a lightly floured surface. Knead lightly, form into a disk, and wrap with plastic wrap. Refrigerate for at least 4 hours or up to overnight.

Preheat the oven to 425°F/220°C.

On a lightly floured surface, roll dough into a circle slightly larger than a 9-in/23-cm pie pan. Fit the dough into the pan and trim excess from the edges. Line the dough with aluminum foil and fill with pie weights or dried beans. Bake for 15 minutes. Remove the crust from the oven and carefully remove foil and weights. Let the crust cool on a wire rack.

To make the filling: Preheat the oven to 400°F/200°C. Line a rimmed baking sheet with aluminum foil. Prick each sweet potato several times with a fork and put on the prepared baking sheet. Bake until tender when pierced with a fork, 40 to 45 minutes. Remove from the oven and let cool to room temperature.

CONTINUED

CRUST

¾ CUP/95 G all-purpose flour

¼ TSP baking powder

¼ TSP kosher salt

6 TBSP/85 G unsalted butter, cut into cubes and chilled

½ CUP/120 ML sour cream

SWEET POTATO FILLING

1 LB/455 G orange-fleshed sweet potatoes

1 CUP/200 G firmly packed brown sugar

½ TSP ground cinnamon

½ TSP ground allspice

¼ TSP grated nutmeg

1 TSP salt

4 eggs

1 CUP/240 ML heavy cream

¼ CUP/60 ML orange juice

4 TBSP/55 G unsalted butter, melted and cooled slightly

Reduce the oven temperature to 350°F/180°C. Scoop the flesh from the sweet potatoes and purée in a food processor. Transfer to a large bowl.

In a small bowl, combine the brown sugar, cinnamon, allspice, nutmeg, and salt, stirring to break up any lumps. Stir the brown sugar mixture into the sweet potatoes. In the same small bowl, whisk together the eggs and cream, add to the sweet potato mixture, and stir to combine. Add the orange juice and the melted butter, and stir to combine.

Pour the filling into the blind baked crust and bake until set in the center, about 45 minutes.

Transfer to a wire rack to let cool completely. Serve at room temperature.

(To make ahead, cover with plastic wrap and refrigerate for up to 2 days.)

SPICED SWEET POTATO BUNDT CAKE

Sweet potatoes and chocolate chips seem like an unlikely combination, but they work really well together. I like to tell myself that the sweet potatoes help make the cake a nutritious snack as well as a sweet one. If you want to gild the lily, drizzle with Chocolate-Chicory Sauce (page 169). If you like baking cakes, it's worth investing in a nice Bundt pan. They're a simple way to make pretty cakes.

Preheat the oven to 350°F/180°C. Butter and flour a 12-cup/ 2.8-L Bundt pan.

In a medium pot, cover the sweet potatoes with water. Bring to a boil, and cook until the potatoes are soft, about 15 minutes. Drain.

In a medium bowl, whisk together the flour, sugar, baking soda, cinnamon, allspice, nutmeg, ginger, and salt.

Using a stand mixer fitted with the paddle attachment, beat the cooked sweet potatoes and eggs on medium speed until smooth. Add the melted butter and beat until combined. Reduce the speed to low, add the flour mixture, and mix just until combined. Remove the workbowl from the mixer and, with a wooden spoon, stir in the chocolate chips. Spoon the batter into the prepared Bundt pan.

Bake until a toothpick or skewer inserted into the center of the cake comes out clean, 40 to 50 minutes. Transfer to a wire rack to let cool completely in the pan, about 1 hour. Loosen the cake from the pan using the tip of a dinner knife, then invert a rack over the pan and turn the cake out onto the rack.

Serve at room temperature.

(To make ahead, cover with plastic wrap and store at room temperature for up to 3 days.)

1½ LB/680 G orange-fleshed sweet potatoes, peeled and cut into large pieces

3⅓ CUPS/420 G all-purpose flour

2 CUPS/400 G sugar

1 TBSP baking soda

1 TBSP ground cinnamon

1 TBSP ground allspice

1 TBSP grated nutmeg

1 TBSP ground ginger

½ TSP kosher salt

4 eggs

1 CUP/225 G unsalted butter, melted and slightly cooled

2 CUPS/340 G chocolate chips

APPLE
BUNDT CAKE
WITH BROWN SUGAR
GLAZE

My Grandma Thomas, my maternal grandmother from Louisiana, made this apple cake every holiday season, and I still have the handwritten recipe that she mailed to me years ago. She was a huge influence on my cooking and my knowledge of food. At one point, she worked for the Louisiana Cooperative Board and distributed healthful, simple recipes to low-income families. She would send me copies of the recipes, and I loved reading them and imagining the flavors. This cake remains one of my favorites. It's so moist that no ice cream is needed.

3½ CUPS/440 G all-purpose flour

1 TSP baking soda

1 TSP ground cinnamon

3 eggs

2 CUPS/400 G granulated sugar

1½ CUPS/360 ML vegetable oil

1 TSP kosher salt

1 LB/455 G firm Granny Smith apples, cored, peeled, and cut into small dice

1 CUP/140 G walnuts, lightly toasted and coarsely chopped [see page 75]

BROWN SUGAR GLAZE

1 CUP/200 G firmly packed brown sugar

½ CUP/115 G unsalted butter

¼ CUP/60 ML whole milk

Preheat the oven to 350°F/180°C. Butter and flour a 12-cup/2.8-L Bundt pan.

In a medium bowl, whisk together the flour, baking soda, and cinnamon.

Using a stand mixer fitted with the paddle attachment, mix the eggs, granulated sugar, oil, and salt on medium speed until combined. Reduce the speed to low, add the flour mixture, and mix until completely moistened. Remove the workbowl from the mixer and, with a wooden spoon, gently fold in the apples and walnuts. Spoon the batter into the prepared Bundt pan.

Bake until a toothpick or skewer inserted into the center of the cake comes out clean, 60 to 75 minutes. Transfer to a wire rack to let cool in the pan for about 15 minutes. Loosen the cake from the pan using the tip of a dinner knife, then invert a rack over the pan and turn the cake out onto the rack. Set the rack on a parchment-lined baking sheet.

To make the glaze: In a saucepan, combine the brown sugar, butter, and milk over high heat. Bring to a boil, and cook, stirring occasionally, until the sugar has completely dissolved, about 5 minutes.

Carefully spoon the glaze over the warm cake. Let cool completely. Serve at room temperature.

(To make ahead, cover with plastic wrap and store at room temperature for up to 3 days.)

BRUCE COX

EXECUTIVE DIRECTOR, ALLIANCE FOR WEST OAKLAND DEVELOPMENT

Works: West Oakland, 30 years

Regular orders: Breakfast tart, blackened catfish

I met Tanya at a city council meeting when we both went asking for funding. She was looking for help in getting Brown Sugar Kitchen opened and I needed money for my nonprofit organization. I teach building trades at a couple of West Oakland schools and am considered an expert on the old Victorian houses in the area. I've helped a lot of kids get jobs working on the new construction in the neighborhood. I had a rough childhood and I could've easily taken a wrong turn, but learning a trade helped to steer me in the right direction. Now it's my turn to help. They give me the roughest kids in the school. I don't believe in babysitting them, but I'm humble enough to understand what they're going through. It can be a challenge, but I'm able to talk to them.

I stop by Brown Sugar Kitchen anytime I'm in the neighborhood. I can't get two steps in the door there without seeing someone I know. Coming to Brown Sugar Kitchen is the highlight of my day. We need more places like it. Look at the diversity of the people Tanya's hired. We both work hard to create jobs for people in the neighborhood. That means a lot.

PINEAPPLE
UPSIDE-DOWN CAKE

This cake reminds me of church bake sales. When I was a kid in upstate New York, I attended a Southern-ish Baptist church. It seemed that there was always one group or another raising funds for uniforms or a field trip. Each person trying to outdo the other with a secret family recipe. Bake sales were an early form of crowdfunding, and the rewards provided immediate gratification.

¾ CUP/170 G unsalted butter, at room temperature

½ CUP/100 G firmly packed brown sugar

1 ripe pineapple, peeled, cored, and cut into ¼-in/6-mm rings or half-moons

1½ CUPS/185 G all-purpose flour

1½ TSP baking powder

¼ TSP kosher salt

1 CUP plus 2 TBSP/225 G granulated sugar

2 eggs plus 1 egg yolk

1 TSP vanilla extract

½ CUP plus 2 TBSP/180 ML buttermilk

Preheat the oven to 350°F/180°C. Butter and flour a 9-in/23-cm round cake pan.

In a small saucepan, combine ¼ cup/55 g of the butter and the brown sugar over low heat; stir until the butter is melted and the sugar has dissolved. Pour the mixture into the prepared cake pan, spreading it into an even layer to cover the bottom. Arrange the pineapple slices on top.

In a small bowl, sift together the flour, baking powder, and salt. Using a stand mixer fitted with the paddle attachment, cream the remaining ½ cup/115 g butter and the granulated sugar on medium speed until light and fluffy, about 5 minutes, scraping down the bowl at least twice. Add the eggs and egg yolk, one at a time, beating well after each addition. Add the vanilla and mix until combined. Reduce speed to low, and add the flour mixture and the buttermilk alternately, in three additions, beginning and ending with the flour.

With a rubber spatula, scrape the batter over the pineapple in the cake pan and spread into an even layer. Bake until a toothpick inserted into the center comes out clean, 50 to 55 minutes.

Let the cake cool in the pan on a wire rack for about 20 minutes. Loosen the cake from the pan using the tip of a thin, sharp knife, then carefully invert the cake onto a flat serving plate. Replace any fruit that might have been left in the pan. Let cool completely. Serve at room temperature.

(The cake is best served the day it is baked, but to make ahead, cover with plastic wrap or store in an airtight container at room temperature for up to 1 day or refrigerate for up to 3 days.)

CARAMEL LAYER CAKE WITH BROWN BUTTER-CARAMEL FROSTING

This is a "company's coming" cake. It's a little extra work, but the results are worth it. Break up the tasks and you'll enjoy the process more. You can bake the cakes two days before, cover them tightly with plastic wrap, and refrigerate them until you need them. The caramel syrup and the browned butter can also be made ahead and stored in airtight jars in the refrigerator. To me, caramel is one of those sweet flavors that I never tire of; it's right up there with chocolate. Its concentrated richness has a slightly bitter edge that makes it almost savory.

5 CUPS/620 G flour

1 TSP baking powder

1¼ CUPS/280 G unsalted butter, at room temperature

2½ CUPS/500 G granulated sugar

2 TSP salt

⅔ CUP/165 ML Caramel Syrup (page 189), cooled

4 eggs

2 TSP vanilla extract

2 CUPS/480 ML whole milk

BROWN BUTTER-CARAMEL FROSTING

¾ CUP/170 G unsalted butter

2¾ CUPS/280 G powdered sugar

½ TSP vanilla extract

½ TSP salt

¼ CUP/60 ML heavy cream, plus more as needed

3 TBSP Caramel Syrup (page 189), cooled

Preheat the oven to 350°F/180°C. Butter and flour two 9-in/23-cm round cake pans.

In a small bowl, whisk together the flour and baking powder. Using a stand mixer fitted with the paddle attachment, cream the butter, granulated sugar, and salt on medium speed until light and fluffy, about 5 minutes, scraping down the bowl at least twice. Drizzle in the cooled caramel syrup and mix just until combined. Add the eggs, one at a time, beating well after each addition. Add the vanilla and mix until combined. Reduce the speed to low, and add the flour mixture and the milk alternately, in three additions, beginning and ending with the flour.

Scrape the batter into the prepared pans. Bake until the sides pull away from the pan and a toothpick stuck into the centers of the cakes comes out clean, about 25 minutes.

Let the cakes cool in the pans on a wire rack for 10 minutes. Invert the cakes onto the rack and cool completely before frosting. (To make ahead, cover the cakes tightly with plastic wrap, and refrigerate for up to 48 hours or freeze for up to 2 weeks. If frozen, thaw the layers before assembling the cake.)

CONTINUED

To make the frosting: In a small, heavy-bottomed saucepan, melt the butter over medium heat. Continue cooking, watching carefully to be sure the butter doesn't burn, until brown specks form on the bottom of the pan. Remove from the heat and strain the melted butter through a fine-mesh sieve to remove any sediment. Let cool to room temperature.

Using a stand mixer fitted with the paddle attachment, combine the brown butter, powdered sugar, vanilla, and salt and mix on medium speed until combined. Reduce the speed to low, slowly pour in the cream and the cooled caramel syrup, and mix until smooth. If the frosting seems too thick, mix in another 1 tbsp cream.

Place one cake layer, bottom-side up, on a cake stand or serving plate. Using an offset spatula, spread the top of the layer with frosting. Place a second cake layer, bottom-side up, on top of the first layer, and frost the top and then the sides with a thin layer of frosting, making sure to cover all the crumbs. Let the cake rest in a cool place until the frosting sets, 30 to 60 minutes. This is called a crumb coat and will help ensure that the final coat of frosting will go on smoothly and evenly.

Spread the remaining frosting over the top and sides of the cake. Cut into slices and serve at room temperature.

(To store any leftovers, press plastic wrap against the cut surfaces of the cake and top with a cake cover or a large bowl for up to 3 days.)

CARAMEL **SYRUP**

In a heavy-bottomed saucepan, combine the sugar and ½ cup/ 120 ml of the water over medium-high heat. When the sugar turns a deep amber color, carefully add the remaining 1 cup/240 ml water. Continue cooking the caramel at a gentle boil until it thickens to a syrup-like consistency, about 15 minutes. Let cool to room temperature. (To make ahead, refrigerate for up to 1 month.)

1 CUP/200 G sugar
1½ CUPS/355 ML water

RED VELVET LAYER CAKE

We put this cake on the counter and start counting down: 5 slices left, 2 slices. It rarely lasts more than an hour. Soon there's nothing left but a plate of red crumbs. I find that I need to perform quality control on this cake a little more than on others, constantly "testing" to make sure it's just right. Okay, it's a weakness. And this is a cake that always looks festive. One of my all-time favorites, this is the cake we served at our wedding. Did I mention that I love this cake?

2½ CUPS/315 G all-purpose flour

1½ CUPS/300 G sugar

1 TBSP natural cocoa powder

1 TSP baking soda

1 TSP kosher salt

2 eggs

1 CUP/240 ML buttermilk

1½ CUPS/360 ML canola oil

2 TBSP red food coloring

1 TSP distilled white vinegar

1 TSP vanilla extract

CREAM CHEESE FROSTING

1 CUP/255 G unsalted butter, at room temperature

1 LB/455 G cream cheese, at room temperature

4 CUPS/400 G powdered sugar, sifted

1 TSP vanilla extract

1 CUP/110 G coarsely chopped walnuts or pecans, toasted (optional, see page 75)

Preheat the oven to 350°F/180°C. Butter and flour two 9-in/23-cm round cake pans.

In the bowl of a stand mixer fitted with the paddle attachment, sift together the flour, sugar, cocoa, baking soda, and salt. In a medium bowl, whisk the eggs, buttermilk, oil, food coloring, vinegar, and vanilla.

With the mixer on low speed, slowly pour the egg mixture into the flour mixture and beat until the batter becomes smooth and ribbon-like, scraping the bowl as needed.

Scrape the batter into the prepared pans and smooth on top. Bake until the sides pull way from the pan and a toothpick stuck into the centers of the cakes comes out clean, 35 to 40 minutes.

Let the cakes cool in the pans on a wire rack for about 10 minutes. Invert the cakes onto the rack to let completely cool before frosting.

(To make ahead, cover the cakes tightly with plastic wrap, and refrigerate for up to 24 hours, or freeze for up to 2 weeks. If frozen, thaw the layers before assembling the cake.)

To make the frosting: Using a stand mixer fitted with the paddle attachment, combine the butter and cream cheese and mix on medium speed until combined. Reduce the speed to low, add the powdered sugar and vanilla, and beat until just combined. Continue mixing, gradually increasing the speed to medium-high, until the frosting is smooth.

Place one cake layer, bottom-side up, on a cake stand or serving plate. Using an offset spatula, spread the top of the layer with about one-third of the frosting. Place the second layer, bottom-side up, on top of the first layer, and spread the remaining frosting over the top and sides of the cake. Press the walnuts (if using) into the sides of the cake.

Refrigerate the cake until ready to serve.

(The cake is best served within 1 day of being baked. To store any leftovers, press plastic wrap against the cut surfaces of the cake and top with a cake cover or a large bowl and store for up to 2 days.)

CHAPTER 7

DRINKS

Sweet tea, lemonade, cocktails spiked with bourbon and mint—these beverages are every bit as essential to the soul food kitchen as fried chicken and biscuits. At Brown Sugar Kitchen, as well as our restaurant B-Side, we offer guests freshly made, cooling drinks that honor my Southern heritage. What follows is a collection of some of my favorite libations—some are cool and refreshing, others comforting and warm; a few have alcohol, others do not. There are classic drinks included here and others that are my own invention.

PERFECTLY MINTED ICED TEA

Sweet tea versus unsweetened tea—that's a tough one. Many people who come to Brown Sugar Kitchen expect Southern-style super-sweet tea. They're happily surprised by our lightly sweetened tea made with agave syrup. We brew the Calypso Mango black tea blend from local producer Mighty Leaf Tea from Marin County, just northwest of Oakland. Use any flavored black tea you like, such as Darjeeling or Earl Grey. Pick your favorite for this very simple recipe.

3 QT/2.8 L water

8 black tea bags

1 bunch fresh mint, top sprigs reserved for garnish

½ CUP/120 ML agave syrup

Ice cubes

In a large saucepan, bring the water to a boil. Remove from the heat and add the tea bags and mint. Steep for 30 minutes. Strain through a fine-mesh sieve into a pitcher or jar and stir in the agave syrup. Let cool to room temperature. Cover and refrigerate until cold, at least 2 hours or up to overnight. Serve in tall glasses over ice, and garnish with the reserved mint sprigs.

MANGO-GINGER
LIMEADE

The tropical combination of mango, lime, and ginger is just the refresher I crave after a day of working in a hot kitchen. You can substitute any fruit you have on hand, such as strawberries, melons, or peeled peaches or nectarines. And on those evenings when you seek serious adult refreshment, try it with vodka, tequila, or rum.

In a blender or food processor, process the mangoes until smooth. In a pitcher or jar, combine the sugar and lime juice, stirring until the sugar dissolves. Add the mango purée, lime zest, water, and ginger and stir until combined. Refrigerate until cold, at least 2 hours or up to overnight. Serve in tall glasses over ice, and garnish with lime wheels.

2 ripe mangoes, peeled, pitted, and cut into chunks

1 CUP/200 G sugar

3 CUPS/720 ML fresh lime juice, 1 TSP lime zest, plus lime wheels for garnish

1½ CUPS/360 ML water

1 TBSP grated fresh ginger

Ice cubes

Ginger Beer

Perfectly Minted Iced Tea

Strawberry Lemonade

Mango-Ginger Limeade

STRAWBERRY LEMONADE

One popular image of the American South includes neighbors spending long afternoons on the front porch sipping sweet iced tea and lemonade. From what I remember of my time spent in Louisiana and Virginia, that's not far from the truth. At Brown Sugar Kitchen, we like to serve lemonade blended with fresh fruit—mango, blackberry, raspberry, and, of course, strawberry are just a few of our favorites. Shuna Lydon, a well-known pastry chef who has cooked all over the Bay Area and New York City, taught us the trick of mixing sugar with zest to make sugar that takes on a more intense lemon flavor.

To make the lemon sugar: In a small bowl, combine the sugar and lemon zest. (To make ahead, refrigerate in an airtight container for up to 3 days.)

In a blender or food processor, combine the lemon sugar and strawberries and process until the sugar is dissolved and the berries are smooth. Transfer to a pitcher, and stir in the lemon juice and water. Cover and refrigerate until cold, at least 2 hours or up to overnight. Serve in tall glasses over ice, and garnish with lemon wedges.

LEMON SUGAR
¾ CUP/150 G sugar
Zest of 2 large lemons

2 CUPS/580 G fresh or frozen strawberries, plus 4 to 6 for garnish
2 CUPS/480 ML fresh lemon juice, plus lemon wedges for garnish
4 CUPS/960 ML water
Ice cubes

GINGER
BEER

Don't be intimidated by making ginger beer from scratch. It's easier than you think and the results more than reward the effort. We use this in our Dark & Stormy cocktail (see facing page), but it's also refreshing on its own poured over ice in a tall glass.

1 CUP/200 G sugar
¼ TSP active dry yeast
2 TBSP grated fresh ginger
1 TBSP fresh lemon juice
Ice cubes

Using a funnel, add the sugar, yeast, ginger, and lemon juice to a 2-qt/2-L plastic bottle. Add enough water to fill about one-quarter full, cap the bottle, and shake a couple of times to mix the ingredients. Add more water to fill the bottle, leaving about 1 in/2.5 cm of empty space at the top. Cap tightly and store at room temperature until the soda is carbonated, 1 to 2 days. Refrigerate at least 1 day or up to 1 month. Strain through a fine-mesh sieve into a pitcher. Serve in tall glasses over ice.

DARK & STORMY

An anomaly in the world of cocktails, the Dark & Stormy is actually a registered trademark that requires the use of Gosling's Black Seal Bermuda Rum. We especially like it made with our own Ginger Beer. It's a fun project that's surprisingly easy. Use store-bought ginger beer, if you like, but don't substitute ginger ale—it's simply not the same.

Fill a tall glass with ice. Add the rum and lime juice, and stir. Top with the ginger beer and garnish with the lime wedge. Serve immediately.

Ice cubes

¼ CUP/60 ML dark rum, such as Gosling's Black Seal

2 TBSP fresh lime juice

¼ CUP/60 ML Ginger Beer (facing page)

Lime wedge for garnish

THE B-SIDE

Our barbecue restaurant, B-Side, is named for the second side of a hit 45 record, the hit, of course, being Brown Sugar Kitchen. We're fortunate that our sophomore effort has turned out to be a success as well. Of course, B also stands for bourbon and barbecue, both beloved in the South. It took some time for us to find the right flavors to embody all that we feel about B-Side, but this drink has it all. If you're unfamiliar with some of the ingredients, the mezcal adds a touch of smokiness, the Gran Classico Bitter brings an herbaceous orange flavor, and the Burlesque lends a floral berry finish. It's a unique combination—and tasting is believing.

Combine the bourbon, mezcal, lemon juice, all three bitters, simple syrup, and ice in a cocktail shaker. Shake until the ingredients are well chilled, about 30 seconds. Strain into a martini glass and serve immediately.

1½ OZ/45 ML **bourbon, such as Buffalo Trace**

½ OZ/15 ML **mezcal**

¾ OZ/22.5 ML **fresh lemon juice**

¼ OZ/7.5 ML **Gran Classico Bitter**

2 DASHES of **Angostura aromatic bitters**

2 DASHES of **Burlesque bitters**

¾ OZ/22.5 ML **Vanilla Simple Syrup (page 204)**

Ice cubes

VANILLA
SIMPLE SYRUP

1 CUP/240 ML water
1 CUP/200 G sugar
1 vanilla bean

In a small heavy-bottomed saucepan, combine the water and sugar. Split the vanilla bean lengthwise, scrape the seeds into the pan, and then add the pod. Bring to a boil and cook, stirring occasionally, until the sugar has completely dissolved, about 2 minutes. Let cool completely and remove and discard pod before using, about 2 hours. (To make ahead, refrigerate in an airtight container for up to 1 month.)

BROWN SUGAR
SANGRIA

I love any recipe that takes ingredients that might otherwise go to waste and turns them into something delicious. This sangria is a perfect example of my waste-not-want-not ethos—combine some extra wine that's been open a little too long with fruit that's edging toward overripe and balance it all with the caramel-like flavor of one of my favorite ingredients, brown sugar. Macerating the fruit overnight in sugar and brandy deepens the flavor and helps avoid sangria that tastes like fruit punch. Add the triple sec just before serving to bring the citrus flavors front and center.

In a 1-gl/3.8-L jar, combine the brown sugar and brandy, stirring to dissolve the sugar. Add the red wine and lemon and orange slices, and refrigerate overnight.

Before serving, stir in the triple sec. Serve in tall glasses, over ice, if desired, garnished with mint sprigs.

1 CUP/200 G firmly packed light brown or raw sugar

½ CUP/120 ML brandy

THREE 750-ml bottles fruity red wine, such as Merlot

3 lemons, thinly sliced

3 oranges, thinly sliced

⅓ CUP/75 ML triple sec

Ice (optional)

Mint sprigs for garnish

CYPRESS SLING

Long before Brown Sugar Kitchen opened its doors, the Cypress freeway ran though West Oakland, dividing the neighborhood in half. Homes were demolished to make way for the freeway, the traffic clogged the area with pollution, and some historians point to it as a factor in the neighborhood's demise. In 1989, the freeway fell during the Loma Prieta earthquake. Many people were injured in the collapse and 43 others died, but out of that tragedy came West Oakland's rebirth. Rather than rebuild the freeway, the residents successfully lobbied for a new thoroughfare. Today the Mandela Parkway is a neighborhood jewel that includes a 14-acre meridian landscaped with native plants. Young families push strollers here, people walk their dogs, and kids ride bikes and skateboards. It's a gathering spot for the community and I'm happy to say the address of Brown Sugar Kitchen. This cocktail, an herbaceous blend of gin, cucumber soda, and thyme, is my way of acknowledging West Oakland's past and a toast to its bright future.

2 OZ/60 ML gin

¾ OZ/22.5 ML **Thyme Syrup** [facing page]

4½ TSP fresh lime juice

Ice cubes

12 OZ/360 ML cucumber soda, such as Dry Soda brand

Thyme sprig for garnish

Combine the gin, thyme syrup, lime juice, and ice in a cocktail shaker. Shake until the ingredients are well chilled, about 30 seconds. Strain into a highball glass filled with ice and top with the cucumber soda. Garnish with a thyme sprig to serve.

THYME **SYRUP**

In a small heavy-bottomed saucepan, combine the water, sugar, and thyme. Bring to a boil and cook, stirring occasionally, until the sugar has completely dissolved, about 2 minutes. Strain though a fine-mesh sieve into a small jar and let cool completely before using, about 2 hours. (To make ahead, refrigerate for up to 1 month.)

1 CUP/240 ML water
1 CUP/200 G sugar
Small bunch fresh thyme

WESTSIDE
JULEP

I discovered mint juleps at the steeplechase races in Charlottesville, Virginia, when I was in college there. Though the races were more of an excuse to socialize than to actually watch the horses, I thought the juleps were a very elegant way to drink bourbon, especially when served in the traditional pewter cups. I've added citrus to bring a little California to this classic Southern cocktail. The name is a nod to our neighborhood in sweet West Oakland.

8 fresh mint leaves, plus mint sprig for garnish

1 TBSP Minted Brown Sugar Syrup (page 210)

⅓ CUP/75 ML bourbon, such as Four Roses

1½ TSP fresh lemon juice

Ice cubes, plus crushed ice for serving

In a cocktail shaker, use a muddler or the handle of a wooden spoon to crush the mint leaves. Add the sugar syrup, bourbon, lemon juice, and ice cubes. Shake to chill the ingredients, about 30 seconds. Strain into a julep cup or a lowball glass filled with crushed ice. Garnish with the mint sprig. Serve immediately.

MINTED BROWN SUGAR SYRUP

1 CUP/240 ML water

1 CUP/200 G firmly packed brown sugar

Leaves from 1 bunch fresh mint, chopped

In a small heavy-bottomed saucepan, combine the water, brown sugar, and mint. Bring to a boil and cook, stirring occasionally, until the sugar has completely dissolved, about 2 minutes. Strain though a fine-mesh sieve into a small jar and let cool completely before using, about 2 hours. (To make ahead, refrigerate for up to 1 month.)

SAMUEL FREDERICKS

OWNER, SAMUEL'S ART GALLERY

Lives: West Oakland, since 2003

Regular order: Cheese grits and eggs

I was living by Lake Merritt for many years, and my wife used to drive through West Oakland on her way from BART. She used to comment that the neighborhood felt like the South to her. It was her idea that we move here. Our home is an Oakland Landmark, an old Victorian known as the Hume-Wilcutt House.

I first heard Tanya when she was interviewed on the radio before Brown Sugar Kitchen opened. She said that she was going to be making biscuits, so I wrote down the address. When the restaurant opened, I came by and it's been a love affair ever since. Now we make it a point to eat here several times a month.

Brown Sugar Kitchen brings people to West Oakland who would otherwise never come here. It's a joy to drive by the restaurant on the weekends and see so many people waiting. More people are discovering that this neighborhood is a little edgy, it's afford-able, and it's a great location that's close to all the freeways.

Before I moved to California, I worked for IBM in upstate New York. Then I ended up out West working for musicians. Somewhere I got the notion that I was going to frame and sell African-American art. That was more than 30 years ago. The last quarter of the twentieth century was an important time for African-American art. *The Cosby Show* put the Black art movement on steroids. It showed us the joy of living with our own art. The timing was perfect for me. I had the wind at my back. I was fortunate enough to see that a piece of art can lift you up. What surrounds you supports you.

SMOKED BUTTERED RUM

I first tasted hot buttered rum at a neighbor's holiday party long before I was of legal drinking age. So warm and delicious, it is, for me, an essential part of the holiday season. Since we're always looking for ways to take advantage of our smoker at B-Side BBQ, we decided to smoke the butter. That light hint of applewood and hickory turns out to be the ideal counterpoint for the sweetness of the rum.

Boiling water

¼ CUP/60 ML dark rum, such as Gosling's Black Seal

1½ TSP mezcal

3 TBSP Spiced Sugar Syrup (facing page)

1 TBSP Smoked Butter (facing page)

Pour boiling water into a 1¼-cup/300-ml mug and let stand until the mug is warmed, about 1 minute. Discard the water.

Add the rum, mezcal, and sugar syrup to the warmed mug and stir. Add the butter to the mug and then fill the mug with boiling water. Stir the mixture vigorously until the butter has melted. Serve immediately.

SPICED SUGAR SYRUP

In a heavy-bottomed saucepan, combine the water, granulated sugar, brown sugar, cinnamon, star anise, vanilla, and nutmeg. Bring to a boil and cook until the sugars have completely dissolved, about 2 minutes. Strain through a fine-mesh sieve into a small jar, and let cool completely before using, about 2 hours. (To make ahead, refrigerate in an airtight container for up to 1 month.)

1 CUP/240 ML water
½ CUP/100 G granulated sugar
½ CUP/100 G firmly packed light brown sugar
1 cinnamon stick
1 star anise
1 TSP vanilla extract
⅛ TSP freshly grated nutmeg

SMOKED BUTTER

Ignite a gas grill, or start a small fire in a charcoal grill. If using a gas grill, wrap wood chips in a piece of aluminum foil to create a package. Punch holes in the foil with a fork. Set the foil package on top of the grill grates. (If using a charcoal grill, place the wood chips directly on the charcoal.)

Put the butter in a small heatproof container and set the container on the grill grates. Cover the grill, and allow the butter to smoke for about 15 minutes. Remove the container from the grill and pour the smoked butter into a small bowl. Refrigerate for at least 1 hour before using. (To make ahead, refrigerate in an airtight container for up to 30 days.)

½ CUP/115 G unsalted butter

CHAI

Making our own chai blend is easy and allows us to adjust the seasonings exactly to our tastes. We encourage you to do the same. While chai is traditionally made with milk, we find it doesn't really need it, but do add milk if you like. A chai latte can be a wonderful thing. This is also delicious served chilled, over ice.

8 CUPS/2 L water

½ CUP/100 G sugar

6 bay leaves, crushed

1 TBSP cardamom pods, crushed

3 cloves

1 cinnamon stick, broken in half

¼ TSP white peppercorns

1 star anise

½ TSP fennel seeds

4 whole allspice

PINCH of cayenne pepper

1½ TSP grated fresh ginger

½ CUP/120 ML dark agave syrup

4 black tea bags, such as Ceylon or English Breakfast

Ice (optional)

In a large saucepan, combine the water, sugar, bay leaves, cardamom, cloves, cinnamon, peppercorns, star anise, fennel seeds, allspice, and cayenne. Bring to a boil, then add the ginger, agave, and tea bags. Remove from the heat and let steep for 2 minutes. Strain through a fine-mesh strainer into a pitcher. Serve warm in coffee mugs, or refrigerate for at least 4 hours and serve over ice in tall glasses.

(To make ahead, refrigerate in an airtight container for up to 1 week. Reheat gently in a saucepan over medium heat.)

HOT
CHOCOLATE

This recipe, a rich blend of chocolate, cream, and milk, is one I learned to make at a café where I worked in Brooklyn, though it always reminds me of Paris. I spent many hours there "renting" a table at one of the local cafés, drinking *chocolat chaud* and imagining the lives of writers, poets, painters, and perhaps even chefs that lingered in those cafés before me.

In a large saucepan, combine the milk, cream, sugar, and cinnamon. Split the vanilla bean in half lengthwise, scrape the seeds into the pan, and then add the pod. Bring to a boil, reduce to a simmer, and whisk in the chocolate and cocoa powder. Turn off heat and let stand for 15 minutes. Strain through a fine-mesh sieve into a pitcher. Serve warm in mugs and top with marshmallows.

(To make ahead, refrigerate in an airtight container for up to 1 week. Reheat gently in a saucepan over low heat until warm.)

4 CUPS/960 ML whole milk

2 CUPS/480 ML heavy cream

¼ CUP/50 G sugar

1 cinnamon stick

1 vanilla bean

10 OZ/280 G bittersweet chocolate, coarsely chopped

¼ CUP/20 G unsweetened cocoa powder

Marshmallows or freshly whipped cream for garnish

ACKNOWLEDGMENTS

This book wouldn't have shaped into a viable story without my tireless book agent, Danielle Svetcov! Thank you, Danielle.

Thank you to the team at Chronicle Books, including Sarah Billingsley and Alice Chau, for your support and vision-sharing. Thank you to the entire staff for all of the BSK love you had long before I knocked on your door.

I would like to thank Jan Newberry for the countless hours of dedication she poured into this project. She immersed herself into my world and my community. She helped create what I hope will be viewed as a memento of my wonderful neighborhood, as well as a heartfelt cookbook.

Thank you to Jody Horton and Kate LeSueur for capturing the priceless and magical moments that happen at 2534 Mandela Parkway.

Thank you to Michael Chabon for not only being a dedicated BSK fan and choosing our little restaurant to host his *Telegraph Avenue* book launch party, but now for writing more beautiful words to introduce this book. Your foreword brought tears to our eyes. Free waffles for life for you, Ayelet, and the kids!

Many thanks to the pioneering visionaries who are also invested in this neighborhood and Brown Sugar Kitchen: Merritt, Kathryn, Steve, Peter and Chrissy, Pat and Bev, Kathy, Elizabeth, Barry, and may Peter D. and Tiffanie K. rest in peace. And then there's the constant supporters who are growing with us, including Ed, Jeremy, Joe, John, Letty, Sarah, and Rob. I can't thank you enough!

And, yes, there's a team of professionals who are also friends that I just can't live without: my attorney, Jonathan; my publicist, Kristen; my make-up artist, Tricia; our "staff" photographer, Lisa; media coach extraordinaire, Paula; Michelle for wardrobe—you all know who you are. Thank you so much!

I would like to thank the staff at both Brown Sugar Kitchen and B-Side BBQ. They are simply the best in the business. Especially Gemma, Rachel, Maria, Shaun, Nathan, Jeremy, Esme, Angel and Tarrence for your long-term commitment. You allowed me to carve out the precious chunks of time that this project demanded. These people are all special, and you need to come in and tell them so!

I would like to thank my amazing customers, who are also the best in the business! Julia! Judy! Chela! Rob! Every day?! Alvin for your "waffle Wednesdays" and so many folks who I see every week that I only know as "2 pieces with a side of grits" or "hash/poached soft." I feel your support and thank you so much! You are the reason Phil and I do what we do. We have the privilege of meeting such a wide cross-section of unique, kind, and hungry folks every day. We value this experience, and the opportunity to share with our customers.

Samuel Fredericks was Oakland's cultural warrior, art historian, our first regular customer, and was a dear friend. We will miss you. Rest in peace.

I would like to thank all my friends who support me, and put up with my ridiculous schedule. Yes, we will go out for that drink . . . soon! Especially Linda, David, and Shiree!

I'm so grateful that I was able to get to know my grandmothers who both passed shortly after my 35th birthday. I had quite a bit of wonderful time with them. They gave me a lot of love and transferred a lot of joy from their kitchens to mine.

Thank you to my mom and dad, Annette and Hollis Holland. You bought me my first Easy-Bake oven and "got the party started." And I'll always cherish my mini kitchen in the garage that you know I was obsessed with! Thank you for organizing your diverse "Gourmet Club" when I was a young, impressionable child. You exposed me to so many different types of cuisine. Food has become my passion, and I am forever grateful for your open-mindedness.

Thank you to my sister, Janelle, for tasting all of my concoctions along the way and for your unconditional support and love in my absence from home, and for your sweet baby daughter (my baby niece and goddaughter), Lyric. You both are my girls, and I love you dearly.

Thank you Surkises. First, to the late Deborah Surkis who accepted me as her daughter-in-law and requested my ribs at her 75th birthday celebration. Thank you to my sisters-in-law Alisa, Colleen, and Elaine, and to my brother-in-law, Dan. I know that I can always count on you for support, and maybe even some recipe testing, too. Thank to Julia, Claire, Ella, and Zelda for being wonderful nieces. You are all so sweet and talented.

Thank you to the icons Leah Chase, Anne Willan, Martha Stewart, and Julia Child. I've been lucky enough to meet you all and hope to make you proud. Thank you to the many chefs and restaurateurs who have inspired me for years, who have been my role models.

Thank you to the city of Oakland. I didn't anticipate that you would become such a prominent figure in my life. You got under my skin, and I fell in love. You support me in such a way that I feel that I have truly found my home.

Finally, I must say thank you to my love, my husband, Phil. He knows the Brown Sugar Kitchen story better than anyone. He supports me and our restaurants in so many ways. When I first met him many years ago, I told him I was going to open a restaurant. He didn't run away. In fact, he embraced the idea, and encouraged me to follow my passion.

Love to all and always cook with soul!

INDEX